THE SELECTED POEMS
OF
KENNETH REXROTH

BOOKS BY KENNETH REXROTH

POEMS

The Collected Shorter Poems
The Collected Longer Poems
Sky Sea Birds Trees Earth House Beasts Flowers
New Poems
The Phoenix and the Tortoise
The Morning Star
Selected Poems

PLAYS

Beyond the Mountains

CRITICISM & ESSAYS

The Alternative Society
American Poetry in the Twentieth Century
Assays
Bird in the Bush
The Classics Revisited
Communalism, from the Neolithic to 1900
The Elastic Retort
With Eye and Ear

TRANSLATIONS

100 Poems from the Chinese
100 More Poems from the Chinese: Love and the Turning Year
Fourteen Poems of O. V. Lubicz-Milosz
Seasons of Sacred Lust: The Selected Poems of Kazuko Shiraishi
   (*with Ikuko Atsumi, John Solt, Carol Tinker, and
   Yasuyo Morita*)
The Burning Heart: Women Poets of Japan
   (*with Ikuko Atsumi*)
The Orchid Boat: The Women Poets of China
   (*with Ling Chung*)
100 French Poems
Poems from the Greek Anthology
100 Poems from the Japanese
100 More Poems from the Japanese
30 Spanish Poems of Love and Exile
Selected Poems of Pierre Reverdy
Li Ch'ing-chao: Complete Poems (*with Ling Chung*)

AUTOBIOGRAPHY

An Autobiographical Novel

EDITOR

The Continuum Poetry Series

KENNETH
REXROTH
SELECTED POEMS

Edited by Bradford Morrow

A New Directions Book

811.52
R32s

The poems in this book have been selected from *The Collected Shorter Poems of Kenneth Rexroth* (1966), *The Collected Longer Poems of Kenneth Rexroth* (1968), *New Poems* (1974), and *The Morning Star* (1979).

The editor wishes to thank Deborah Baker, Morgan Gibson, Peter Glassgold, Linda Hamalian, James Laughlin, Leslie Miller, and Carol Tinker for useful suggestions they made during the preparation of this book.

Manufactured in the United States of America
First published clothbound and as New Directions Paperbook 581 in 1984
Published simultaneously in Canada by George J. McLeod Ltd., Toronto

Library of Congress Cataloging in Publication Data
Rexroth, Kenneth, 1905–1982
    Selected poems.
    (A New Directions Book)
    Includes index.
    I. Morrow, Bradford, 1951–   .   II. Title.
PS3535.E923A6   1984   811'.52   84–9972
ISBN 0–8112–0916–4
ISBN 0–8112–0917–2 (pbk.)

New Directions Books are published for James Laughlin by New Directions Publishing Corporation, 80 Eighth Avenue, New York 10011

Contents

INTRODUCTION

In H. G. Wells' prologue to Kenneth Rexroth's favorite childhood book, *The Research Magnificent*, the idealistic, brilliant, and rather unbalanced protagonist, William Porphyry Benham, is described as a man who was led into adventure by an idea. This idea took possession of Porphyry's imagination "quite early in life, it grew with him and changed with him, it interwove at last completely with his being." The idea was simple. Life, he thought, must be lived nobly and to the utmost limits; a man must realize something out of his existence: "a flame, a jewel, a splendour." To the precocious thirteen-year-old Rexroth what a heady and marvelous blueprint for life this must have been. Unlike Porphyry, however, whose lifelong research was left crammed in bureau drawers and dozens of patent boxes, as an "indigestible aggregation" of notes for an unwritten book, Rexroth spent the nearly six decades that followed his first reading of *The Research Magnificent* amassing a polymath knowledge that would surpass that of any other American poet of the century (Pound included), while at the same time honing his writing to a simple and direct style that most resembled his own everyday speech (like Williams). As a result he is one of our most readable and yet complex poets. And, like William Porphyry Benham, there was little that didn't interest him enough to at least attempt to master it.

Peripateticism and a spirit free of prejudice, rather than a focus on the local, are the twin bases of Rexroth's fundamentally American personality. (It is a combination that would in the 1950s influence members of the Beat generation who gathered around Rexroth in San Francisco and made of him that Movement's unwilling father figure.) Born in South Bend, Indiana, on December 22, 1905, and raised in Chicago, Elkhart, Battle Creek, and Toledo, it would have been very natural for him to have developed an art whose themes derived from a pure Midwestern upbringing. But, if we are to believe the exuberant portrait of his youth set out in his *An Autobiographical Novel*, his precocity and a bohemian attitude toward life were already in full blossom by the time he was in his teens.

A pioneer brand of rational empiricism and pietistic radicalism ran deep in the family's history. Of German-American ancestry, both of Rexroth's grandfathers showed politically dissident tendencies, and descended themselves from the Schwenkfelders, a heterodox sect (whose beliefs are substantially the Quakers') that arrived in America before William Penn. While by the turn of the present century the sectarian religious cast of the Schwenkfelders had within Rexroth's family been transformed, the "radical ethical social impulse" remained, and produced in Rexroth's forefathers an inherited, almost instinctive radicalism. Indeed, his paternal grandfather George voted straight Socialist tickets and always read the Socialist papers before finally declaring himself an Anarchist in his last years. The familial climate in which Rexroth was reared nurtured self-sufficiency, self-respect, as well as a strong sense of ethical activism and "a philosophy of caste responsibility":

> I learned that other people were not as we were, but slightly demented, and demented in such a way that they could easily become dangerous. And I learned that we, as more responsible members of society who knew better, had to take care of them as though they were sick. In fact, I gained the impression then that the society which lay over against my family—*les autres*, as the French say—was a helpless and dangerous beast that we had to tend to and save from its own irrationality. I rather doubt if anything in life has ever caused me to give up this attitude.

This basic Socialist principle prompted in Rexroth the notion that all learning had inherent societal ramifications. It was a central criterion in his mother's pedagogic system that each and every bit of information her son learned must not be an abstract thing mastered for its own sake, but was studied for keeps, was a tool meant to be applied in society on a daily basis.

Rexroth's father, Charles, was a moderately successful pharmacist. His mother, Delia, oversaw most of her only son's education herself, rather than sending him to school. She instructed him in elementary arithmetic, history, astronomy, and the natural sciences, and taught him to read by the age of four, at which time she procured for him a library card. His parents helped him set up a small laboratory; even his toys were Froebellian and Montessorian, carefully selected for color and design. When he wasn't reading or studying he spent much of his time outdoors, was an avid hunter and, with his mother's help, learned the rudiments of botany and zoology. Although he has described his childhood as fundamentally Edwardian, various eccentric circumstances, such as his befriending at the age of five or six an elderly American Indian, Billy Sunlight, who lived on the Rexroth's property in a remodeled chicken coop, gave it character and quality that would elude any such rubric.

The ranging private education Rexroth received from his mother stood him in good stead after he was orphaned in 1918. His parents' marriage had begun to falter several years before this; his father's business experienced a reversal in fortune, and he began to drink heavily. Delia Rexroth died in June 1916—not three years before Charles finally suffered a miserable, painful death as a result of acute alcoholism. Upon moving in with his aunt in Chicago (see "The Bad Old Days"), Rexroth decided he would be a writer and an artist, and his education toward those ends began in earnest. He attended the Chicago Art Institute and Bush Conservatory, but soon became "a consummate master in the art of plausible hooky." An alternative educational system now insinuated itself:

> More than any of the official education and cultural institutions my favorite school was the Washington Park Bug Club . . . Here until midnight could be heard passionate exponents of every variety of human lunacy. There were Anarchist-Single-Taxers, British-Israelites, self-annointed archbishops of the American Catholic Church, Druids, Anthroposophists, and geologists who had proven the world was flat or that the surface of the earth was the inside of a hollow sphere, and people who were in communication with the inhabitants of Mars, Atlantis, and Tibet, severally and sometimes simultaneously. Besides, struggling for a hearing was the whole body of orthodox heterodoxy—Socialists, communists (still with a small "c"), IWWs, De Leonites,

Anarchists, Single Taxers (separately, not in contradictory combination), Catholic Guild Socialists, Schopenhauerians, Nietzscheans—of whom there were quite a few—Stinerites, and what were later to be called Fascists.

At the center of the Bug Club was a William Porphyry Benham come to life, one Judge Walter Freeman Cooling. Under the judge's Socratean wing came a footloose fourteen-year-old who had already digested more books than most people read in a lifetime. Cooling advanced to Rexroth a whimsical theory of the universe which tied together an intellectually rigorous bundle of sources that included the Finnish epic *Kalevala*, Migne's *Patrologia Latinae* and *Graecae*, the *Pirke Aboth*, Homer, the *Zend Avesta*, St. Bonaventura, Jacob Boehme, etc. Rexroth was not drawn into adopting the judge's bizarre polyphilosophic and cosmological system, but the experience was determinative in that it introduced him to the possibilities of autodidacticism and dissent: "With the intelligence of an Aristotle or an Aquinas, [Cooling] disagreed all along the line with all organized thought." Also, less inclined than ever to rejoin his contemporaries in school, he started reading every author the judge happened to mention, and *in toto*. He read the *Sacred Books of the East*. He tried to learn Egyptian. He wrote a play about the heretic king Ikhnaton. Tyndall, Haeckel, Clerk Maxwell, Lyell, Darwin, Mendel, and Faraday were consumed, as were Turgenev, James, Melville, Flaubert, Sainte-Beuve, Dostoevsky, Jack London. Pound's *Cathay* introduced him to Chinese literature. He read straight through the Aldine poets. As a result of this omnivorous and eccentric reading list (the student who wishes to know which books remained important to him in the end is referred to *The Classics Revisited*, in which he appraises sixty key texts) Rexroth was not "converted to the deliquescence of orthodoxy and heterodoxy, so characteristic of our time," but was inoculated against it:

> The radical disbelief which has been characteristic of all my contemporaries I shared from the beginning, but I was never led by it to embrace any of the extraordinary follies which were to become fashionable in intellectual circles in the

next thirty or forty years. I have known Socialist-Realist novelists who religiously consulted the astrology column in the daily newspapers every morning before breakfast. The whole Socialist movement after the First War, led by Frank Harris and Upton Sinclair, embraced the Abrams electronic diagnosis machine. Twenty years later, after the Second War, the reborn Anarchist movement committed suicide in the orgone boxes of Wilhelm Reich. Anyone who had taken a course in high school physics would have known that this stuff was arrant nonsense but the trouble was that these people had lost belief in high school physics along with their belief in capitalism or religion.

At the same time, he began circulating among musicians, artists, anarchists, gangsters, and the considerable human jetsam of radical bohemian Chicago. He tried his hand at numerous jobs, began to paint large abstract canvases, and followed his girlfriend Shirley Johnson to Northampton (see "When We with Sappho") and, finally, to New York. He attended classes at the New School for Social Research and the Art Students League. Living in a brownstone commune on West 13th Street in Greenwich Village, he encountered Marsden Hartley, Mark Tobey, Michael Gold, William Gropper, and others. He briefly met Sacco and Vanzetti and became involved with the Wobblies' labor movement. It is an improbable picaresque, played out against an America that was on the verge of the terrific social upheaval of the twenties, that would form a personality Whitmanesque in its all-embraciveness and Thoreauvian in its attention to detail.

A generation before it became *de rigeur* among bohemians, and two full generations before it was enshrined as a normal activity for bourgeoise collegiates, Rexroth began to hitchhike the length and breadth of the country, sampling different lifestyles, supporting himself as a workaway and occasionally even panhandling when the funds went dry. He drifted from coast to coast and worked every conceivable kind of job (see "A Living Pearl"). He shipped out of Hoboken as a mess steward and got as far as Paris (where he met Aragon, Tzara, Soupault, Cendrars, among others) and down to Buenos Aires. Thirty years before Jack Duluoz set out, he hitched and railed to Mexico City and Oaxaca. At the end of this odyssey he returned to Chicago, resolved to marry; three or four women turned him down before he met a young commercial artist, Andrée Dutcher (born Myrtle Shaefer), whom he married in 1927. Of the four books she had read with enthusiasm in her childhood, it is not surprising that one was *The Research Magnificent*.

In both his autobiography and the poetry Rexroth details the joyous first years they spent together. They painted and read; his poetry was beginning to be published in *Blues, Pagany, Morada,* and elsewhere. As an impromptu honeymoon they hitchhiked to Seattle, and proceeded to hike down the rugged Pacific Northwest coastline until they reached San Francisco, broke. It was a significant turning point in Rexroth's life, for although he found the city intellectually provincial—"Everybody we met considered George Sterling the greatest poet since Dante"—this was to become his home for the next forty years. By the time Andrée died, in October 1940, after a lifelong struggle with epilepsy, Rexroth had become an active member of its political and literary community. Within the decade that followed the outbreak of the war, Frank Norris and George Sterling would be relegated to their proper places as Rexroth laid the groundwork for what was to become the San Francisco Renaissance.

At a Nurses Union meeting he met Marie Cass, whom he married in 1941. A Conscientious Objector to the war, Rexroth worked as an attendant in a psychiatric ward. Their home became not only a meeting place for anarchist and antiwar meetings, as well as literary readings, but a secret convalescent shelter for Japanese seeking to escape internment camps:

> The whole evacuation completely disaffiliated me from the American capitalist state and from the State as such. From then on I've seen very little in American official policy and behavior to be proud of, and Hiroshima, Nagasaki and Vietnam finished the job.

In What Hour, Rexroth's first book of poems, had come out in 1940, and his long poem "The Phoenix and the Tortoise" (published in a book of the same title by New Directions in 1944) voices this same attitude of disaffiliation.

After the war, Rexroth worked off and on as a literary journalist; he wrote more poetry and worked on the series of plays in *Beyond the Mountains*. In 1949, with the appearance of a collection of juvenalia—*The Art of Worldly Wisdom* (published by James Decker, whose murder at the time of publication precluded its being very widely distributed)—his marriage dissolved. Shortly thereafter he married Marthe Larsen, with whom he had two daughters, Mary and Katherine. Marthe was his traveling companion through Europe, documented in *The Dragon and the Unicorn* (1952), and is the subject of some of his finest love poems, included in *In Defense of the Earth* in 1956 (see, "Marthe Away" and "A Dialogue of Watching"). Five years after his divorce in 1961 from Marthe, he moved to Montecito, just south of Santa Barbara, where he later married the poet Carol Tinker; they resided there until his death in June 1982. Always a poet of love within the relationship of holy matrimony (and, invariably, within the realm of nature), each of his four wives may be seen as touchstones through which his philosophy of sacrament and communal love is comprehended. Like burning lights, epiphanal moments passed with each served as mnemonic sparks against which he could measure his own life. Perhaps the most remarkable example of this is the beautiful "Kings River Canyon" passage in "Andrée Rexroth" (*The Signature of All Things*).

Throughout the fifties, Rexroth continued his radical political activities, though his confidence in the Anarchist movement wavered before the memories of his beloved Wobblies, whom he considered purer and more effectual. This position is evident in *The Dragon and the Unicorn*, and in several shorter poems, such as "For Eli Jacobson." Thus, more time was committed to fulfilling his self-assigned role as arbiter of the literary scene in San Francisco; his Potrero Hill rooms were quickly becoming the heart of a growing movement. With the help of Robert Duncan, Madeline Gleason, and Ruth Witt-Diamant, the San Francisco Poetry Center was founded, which for a time attracted writers as well known as Dylan Thomas, W. H. Auden, and William Carlos Williams to give readings. Through articles and on his own KPFA radio program, Rexroth tirelessly brought poets like Duncan, Lamantia, Levertov, Snyder, Ferlinghetti,

Everson, to public attention. When, in 1953, Dylan Thomas died, he wrote the remarkable "Thou Shalt Not Kill," which is widely considered to be the forerunner to, if not the model for, Allen Ginsberg's "Howl." Elegiac in its purpose, this long poem (which he read in clubs to the accompaniment of jazz—Rexroth, Patchen, and Ferlinghetti were the pioneers of this form of performance poetry) remains one of the most incriminating and relentless attacks on the destructive evils of the State ever written.

By the early sixties Rexroth had grown disenchanted with the literary scene he had helped engender: he considered the bohemian lifestyle of the Beats merely a veneer, more a sartorial, pharmaceutical, and gastronomic change than an internal, spiritual revolution. With his famous statement, "An entymologist is not a bug," he severed (though never lived down) his connection with the Beats.

While he had already translated poetry from Chinese and Japanese (as well as French, Italian, Latin, and Greek) this last period of his life is marked by five extended visits to Kyoto, and an increased interest in Buddhism. This inward turn culminated in the Marichiko poems, which were written pseudonymously as "translations" of a young Japanese woman poet; a narrative of love won and lost, these compressed poems achieve, at the end of Rexroth's life, a passionate lyricism equal to his early work, and reveal a spirit still perceptive and elastic. As his reputation as a scholar-critic grew with the publication of a series of prose books—*The Alternative Society, The Bird in the Bush, Assays, American Poetry in the Twentieth Century, Eye and Ear, The Classics Revisited*—so grew his esteem as a translator. Despite this critical output a lifetime of antiacademic pronouncements assured his being seldom taught in university classrooms and, as a consequence, his reputation as a poet drifted into a limbo. As prescient and sparkling as the criticism is, however, it is as a poet that a final assessment of his great achievement must be made.

Rexroth's art works by a technique of self-effacement. His diction and line appear to be effortless, organic, inevitable, without seam. The lack of ostentation he ascribes to his pietistic background finds as its formal companion this straightforward prosody. Still, to dissect and describe how his line, ostensibly so simple on the surface, actually works would be as difficult to do as explain Williams' variable foot: and Rexroth's was surely a less self-consciously developed art.

The longer, philosophical poems operate quite successfully within the same set of technical values as the shorter, lyrical poems. It is at least in part a function of Rexroth's antielitist politics that he never veers too far from a polished colloquial syntax—that of an experienced, unaffected, worldly man speaking. One is conducted through the seemingly spontaneous rhythms toward meaning. Like Blake, Whitman, and Lawrence, such formal directness of language functions in perfect symmetry with an embracing, mystical philosophy which thrusts the manners of that language out and away, almost into palpability. Consider the variety of cadence and verbal tone in the opening lines of "Floating":

> Our canoe idles in the idling current
> Of the tree and vine and rush enclosed
> Backwater of a torpid midwestern stream;
> Revolves slowly, and lodges in the glutted
> Waterlilies. We are tired of paddling.
> All afternoon we have climbed the weak current,
> Up dim meanders, through woods and pastures,
> Past muddy fords where the strong smell of cattle
> Lay thick across the water; singing the songs
> Of perfect, habitual motion; ski songs,
> Nightherding songs, songs of the capstan walk,
> The levee, and the roll of the voyageurs.

For all its rhythmic diversity the lines do not vary beyond nine to eleven syllables (two thirds of the passage is comprised of hendecasyllables); there are four or five stresses per line, mostly four. Yet by unstrained employment of different punctuation, enjambment, and variable balancing of syllabic stresses Rexroth invokes in the reader an actual physical feeling, the sensation of being in this idle canoe, buffeted by irregular, lazy currents, exhausted but alert. It is a remarkable achievement of form, and is carried off with effortless sanguinity. The final four lines constitute such a balance of differing weights—the second line triadic, the third of almost equal proportions mounted on the fulcrum of that comma and balanced out from the middle by the repeated "songs, songs"—they can be compared to a Calder mobile. Similarly, line-breaks are commonly intensified in Rexroth's work by intuitively perfect serializations of the various parts of speech:

> California rolls into
> Sleepy summer, and the air
> Is full of the bitter sweet
> Smoke of the grass fires burning
> On the San Francisco hills.

We see in the terminal positions of these opening lines of "Delia"—each of which has exactly seven syllables—movement from preposition to noun to adjective (though at first appearance "sweet" reads curiously like a substantive, until the eye moves back to the beginning of the next line and reads "smoke"—making "sweet" adjectival) to gerundial verb to noun. Thus the various points of stress, as one moves down through the lines of the single sentence, are here accomplished less by sheer rhythm than the grammatical expectations felt in each end-word, and the consequent "weight" intuited by the reader in those words.

None of these effects is possible, of course, in a verse that suppresses linear syntax. It is for this reason, as much as any other, that Rexroth abandoned the asyntactical techniques (cubist in origin) of the "half decade of foreboding—1927–1932," most of which were published in *The Art of Worldly Wisdom* in 1949. Although he proposed that the elements of his cubist verse (see "Prolegomenon to a Theodicy") "are as simple as the elementary shapes of a cubist painting and the total poem is as definite and apprehensible as the finished picture," it was the measured, syntactical line of "Floating" and "Delia" he was to develop and largely use from the thirties on. Even in the later poems in *The Heart's Garden, The Garden's Heart, On Flower Wreath Hill,* and *The Silver Swan*—so thoroughly influenced by Japanese and Chinese models (after Waley and Pound, Rexroth was the great bringer of East Asian poetry into our culture)—he maintains much the same voice and cadences and line of the earlier work.

The simplicity of exact pronouncement may allow for particularly complex thought. Precision of fact in observation, as well as in syntax or form, is perhaps nowhere more evident than in Rexroth's crucial booklength poem, *The Dragon and the Unicorn*. That this poem is now so seldom read, even by Rexroth aficionados and practitioners of the craft of poetry, troubled Rexroth, and depressed him. For in *The Dragon and the Unicorn* we find the most complete formulation of his personal, mystical philosophy, the most extensive indictment of Western civilization (comparable to, if not as fiery and incantatory as "Thou Shalt Not Kill"), and perhaps the closest approximation to his speaking voice there is in his poetical works. (*An Autobiographical Novel* is the most perfect mirror to Rexroth's spoken word, as it was dictated, and edited only enough to get it past Doubleday's libel lawyers.) Set as a running travelog of his year-long journey through Wales, England, France, Italy, Switzerland, and back to America, *The Dragon and the Unicorn* is a meditation on the nature of love, of time and knowledge, of will and the responsibilities of the self-defining individual, of community (the moral opposite of the collective, the State), and ethics. Juxtapositions are abrupt; the life of the traveler's mind is pingponged against crisply drawn episodes on the road—the latter of which are in turn ribald, poignant, engaging, scientific, very opinionately lived moments. Together the contemplation and the travelog comprise what Rexroth himself has suggested is a Whitmanesque "interior autobiography." And nowhere in his work is the dictum "Epistomology is moral" more intricately played out than this poem.

However important *The Dragon and the Unicorn* may be for one hoping to gain some understanding of Rexroth's general philosophy, there is little doubt that his reputation as a poet rests, at least for the present, more on his love and nature poems (too, on his translations from Chinese and Japanese which, for lack of space, I was unable to include in this selection).

Clearly, he has written some of the most beautiful love poems in the century. His lyric celebrates not merely the disembodied metaphysic nor simply the corporeal erotic, but a synthetic and human whole, composed of both these elements. As a religious poet, Rexroth's love poems are primarily of conjugal love:

Let me celebrate you. I
Have never known anyone
More beautiful than you. I
Walking beside you, watching
You move beside me, watching
That still grace of hand and thigh.
Watching your face change with words
You do not say, watching your
Solemn eyes as they turn to me,
Or turn inward, full of knowing,
Slow or quick, watching your full
Lips part and smile or turn grave,
Watching your narrow waist, your
Proud buttocks in their grace . . .

Fundamentally sacramental, seldom does the poet's contemplation of his love of his wife distinguish between body and soul. In the above passage from "A Dialogue of Love" (written for Rexroth's third wife, Marthe) the usual dichotomy between the observing mind and the tactile flesh is consciously played down: each reflects the other. In an earlier poem, "Between Myself and Death," the dichotomy is altogether erased:

It is wonderful to watch you,
A living woman in a room
Full of frantic sterile people,
And think of your arching buttocks
Under your velvet evening dress,
And the beautiful fire spreading
From your sex, burning flesh and bone,
The unbelievably complex
Tissues of your brain all alive
Under your coiling, splendid hair.

I like to think of you naked.
I put your naked body
Between myself alone and death.

It is the most original and persuasive synthesis of transcendent metaphysical and erotic verse written by an American poet this century.

As a constant backdrop to most of Rexroth's poems, whether travelog, amatory, or meditative, is the immutable presence of nature. Majestic constellations, always wheeling yet always locked in set patterns, embody as heavenly analogues a philosophy of a universe in which all things are ineluctable, unending, linked in a certain process of generation, collapse, rebirth. The moon in its phases is a salient and predominant symbol-charged globe, so often encountered as it walks across the night sky, above the mountains, in many of these poems. Rexroth was a skilled camper and rock-climber, and spent every moment he could manage up in the Sierras, away from the feverish meetings, the readings, the work of the city. Indeed, in the thirties he wrote a full-length book about the subject, *Camping in the Western Mountains*, which was never published. The mountains were his refuge, and it was by the refreshing and, for him, mystical communion with nature that his spirit, and access to his linguistic gift, was most freed.

The poems I have selected represent nearly sixty years' work. For the most part I have followed chronological publication of the poems in books, beginning with the selection from *In What Hour* and ending with work from *The Morning Star*, which collected three shorter books: *The Silver Swan, On Flower Wreath Hill,* and *The Love Poems of Marichiko*. Textually the poems follow the versions given in *The Collected Longer Poems* and *The Collected Shorter Poems*, although I have restored the original title of one of the "Marthe poems" from *In Defense of the Earth*.

The exceptions to this chronological ordering are from two long early poems which are included at the end of this selection. "The Homestead Called Damascus" Rexroth composed in his late teens; it remained unpublished until 1957 when *The Quarterly Review of Literature* brought it out accompanied by an illuminating essay by Lawrence Lipton. Indeed, it wasn't finally published in book form until 1962, when New Directions included it in its World Poets Series. Similarly, his long cubist poem, "A Prolegomenon to a Theodicy," was written in the late 1920s, and was published in an abridged and bowdlerized version in Louis Zukofsky's *An "Objectivists" Anthology* in 1932. The piece was to have appeared in textually complete form in the 1942 Decker edition of *The Art of Worldly Wisdom*, but only a few dozen copies got into circulation. A reissue by The Golden Goose Press in 1957 added Rexroth's lively introduction but due to a small press run and poor distribution it gained few new readers for the poem. Again, it was not until *The Collected Longer Poems* came out in 1966 that this juvenile work truly enjoyed a general circulation. Shorter poems, such as "The Thin Edge of Your Pride," which were also written during this early period but not collected in book form until later, are presented within the context of collections in which they first appeared.

Bradford Morrow
New York City, March 1984

ON WHAT PLANET

Uniformly over the whole countryside
The warm air flows imperceptibly seaward;
The autumn haze drifts in deep bands
Over the pale water;
White egrets stand in the blue marshes;
Tamalpais, Diablo, St. Helena
Float in the air.
Climbing on the cliffs of Hunter's Hill
We look out over fifty miles of sinuous
Interpenetration of mountains and sea.

Leading up a twisted chimney,
Just as my eyes rise to the level
Of a small cave, two white owls
Fly out, silent, close to my face.
They hover, confused in the sunlight,
And disappear into the recesses of the cliff.

All day I have been watching a new climber,
A young girl with ash blond hair
And gentle confident eyes.
She climbs slowly, precisely,
With unwasted grace.
While I am coiling the ropes,
Watching the spectacular sunset,
She turns to me and says, quietly,
"It must be very beautiful, the sunset,
On Saturn, with the rings and all the moons."

REQUIEM FOR THE SPANISH DEAD

The great geometrical winter constellations
Lift up over the Sierra Nevada,
I walk under the stars, my feet on the known round earth.
My eyes following the lights of an airplane,
Red and green, growling deep into the Hyades.
The note of the engine rises, shrill, faint,
Finally inaudible, and the lights go out
In the southeast haze beneath the feet of Orion.

As the sound departs I am chilled and grow sick
With the thought that has come over me. I see Spain
Under the black windy sky, the snow stirring faintly,
Glittering and moving over the pallid upland,
And men waiting, clutched with cold and huddled together,
As an unknown plane goes over them. It flies southeast
Into the haze above the lines of the enemy,
Sparks appear near the horizon under it.
After they have gone out the earth quivers
And the sound comes faintly. The men relax for a moment
And grow tense again as their own thoughts return to them.

I see the unwritten books, the unrecorded experiments,
The unpainted pictures, the interrupted lives,
Lowered into the graves with the red flags over them.
I see the quick gray brains broken and clotted with blood,
Lowered each in its own darkness, useless in the earth.
Alone on a hilltop in San Francisco suddenly
I am caught in a nightmare, the dead flesh
Mounting over half the world presses against me.

Then quietly at first and then rich and full-bodied,
I hear the voice of a young woman singing.
The emigrants on the corner are holding
A wake for their oldest child, a driverless truck

Broke away on the steep hill and killed him,
Voice after voice adds itself to the singing.
Orion moves westward across the meridian,
Rigel, Bellatrix, Betelgeuse, marching in order,
The great nebula glimmering in his loins.

AUTUMN IN CALIFORNIA

Autumn in California is a mild
And anonymous season, hills and valleys
Are colorless then, only the sooty green
Eucalyptus, the conifers and oaks sink deep
Into the haze; the fields are plowed, bare, waiting;
The steep pastures are tracked deep by the cattle;
There are no flowers, the herbage is brittle.
All night along the coast and the mountain crests
Birds go by, murmurous, high in the warm air.
Only in the mountain meadows the aspens
Glitter like goldfish moving up swift water;
Only in the desert villages the leaves
Of the cottonwoods descend in smoky air.
   Once more I wander in the warm evening
Calling the heart to order and the stiff brain
To passion. I should be thinking of dreaming, loving, dying,
Beauty wasting through time like draining blood,
And me alone in all the world with pictures
Of pretty women and the constellations.
But I hear the clocks in Barcelona strike at dawn
And the whistles blowing for noon in Nanking.
I hear the drone, the snapping high in the air
Of planes fighting, the deep reverberant
Grunts of bombardment, the hasty clamor
Of anti-aircraft.
                    In Nanking at the first bomb,
A moon-faced, willowy young girl runs into the street,
Leaves her rice bowl spilled and her children crying,
And stands stiff, cursing quietly, her face raised to the sky.

3

Suddenly she bursts like a bag of water,
And then as the blossom of smoke and dust diffuses,
The walls topple slowly over her.
                              I hear the voices
Young, fatigued and excited, of two comrades
In a closed room in Madrid. They have been up
All night, talking of trout in the Pyrenees,
Spinoza, old nights full of riot and sherry,
Women they might have had or almost had,
Picasso, Velasquez, relativity.
The candlelight reddens, blue bars appear
In the cracks of the shutters, the bombardment
Begins again as though it had never stopped,
The morning wind is cold and dusty,
Their furloughs are over. They are shock troopers,
They may not meet again. The dead light holds
In impersonal focus the patched uniforms,
The dog-eared copy of Lenin's Imperialism,
The heavy cartridge belt, holster and black revolver butt.
    The moon rises late over Mt. Diablo,
Huge, gibbous, warm; the wind goes out,
Brown fog spreads over the bay from the marshes,
And overhead the cry of birds is suddenly
Loud, wiry, and tremulous.

AUGUST 22, 1939

"... when you want to distract your mother from the discouraging
soulness, I will tell you what I used to do. To take her for a long walk
in the quiet country, gathering wildflowers here and there, resting under
the shade of trees, between the harmony of the vivid stream and the
tranquillity of the mother-nature, and I am sure she will enjoy this
very much, as you surely will be happy for it. But remember always,
Dante, in the play of happiness, don't use all for yourself only, but
down yourself just one step, at your side and help the weak ones that
cry for help, help the prosecuted and the victim; because they are
your friends; they are the comrades that fight and fall as your father
and Bartolo fought and fell yesterday, for the conquest of the joy of

What is it all for, this poetry,
This bundle of accomplishment
Put together with so much pain?
Twenty years at hard labor,
Lessons learned from Li Po and Dante,
Indian chants and gestalt psychology;
What words can it spell,
This alphabet of one sensibility?
The pure pattern of the stars in orderly progression,
The thin air of fourteen-thousand-foot summits,
Their Pisgah views into what secrets of the personality,
The fire of poppies in eroded fields,
The sleep of lynxes in the noonday forest,
The curious anastomosis of the webs of thought,
Life streaming ungovernably away,
And the deep hope of man.
The centuries have changed little in this art,
The subjects are still the same.
"For Christ's sake take off your clothes and get into bed,
We are not going to live forever."
"Petals fall from the rose,"
We fall from life,
Values fall from history like men from shellfire,
Only a minimum survives,
Only an unknown achievement.
They can put it all on the headstones,
In all the battlefields,
"Poor guy, he never knew what it was all about."
Spectacled men will come with shovels in a thousand years,
Give lectures in universities on cultural advances, cultural lags.
A little more garlic in the soup,
A half-hour more in bed in the morning,
Some of them got it, some of them didn't;
The things they dropped in their hurry
Are behind the glass cases of dusky museums.

This year we made four major ascents,
Camped for two weeks at timberline,
Watched Mars swim close to the earth,
Watched the black aurora of war
Spread over the sky of a decayed civilization.
These are the last terrible years of authority.
The disease has reached its crisis,
Ten thousand years of power,
The struggle of two laws,
The rule of iron and spilled blood,
The abiding solidarity of living blood and brain.
They are trapped, beleaguered, murderous,
If they line their cellars with cork
It is not to still the pistol shots,
It is to insulate the last words of the condemned.
"Liberty is the mother
Not the daughter of order."
"Not the government of men
But the administration of things."
"From each according to his ability,
Unto each according to his needs."
We could still hear them,
Cutting steps in the blue ice of hanging glaciers,
Teetering along shattered arêtes.
The cold and cruel apathy of mountains
Has been subdued with a few strands of rope
And some flimsy iceaxes,
There are only a few peaks left.
Twenty-five years have gone since my first sweetheart.
Back from the mountains there is a letter waiting for me.
"I read your poem in the New Republic.
Do you remember the undertaker's on the corner,
How we peeped in the basement window at a sheeted figure
And ran away screaming? Do you remember?
There is a filling station on the corner,
A parking lot where your house used to be,
Only ours and two other houses are left.
We stick it out in the noise and carbon monoxide."
It was a poem of homesickness and exile,
Twenty-five years wandering around

In a world of noise and poison.
She stuck it out, I never went back,
But there are domestic as well as imported
Explosions and poison gases.
Dante was homesick, the Chinese made an art of it,
So was Ovid and many others,
Pound and Eliot amongst them,
Kropotkin dying of hunger,
Berkman by his own hand,
Fanny Baron biting her executioners,
Mahkno in the odor of calumny,
Trotsky, too, I suppose, passionately, after his fashion.
Do you remember?
What is it all for, this poetry,
This bundle of accomplishment
Put together with so much pain?
Do you remember the corpse in the basement?
What are we doing at the turn of our years,
Writers and readers of the liberal weeklies?

TOWARD AN ORGANIC PHILOSOPHY

SPRING, COAST RANGE

The glow of my campfire is dark red and flameless,
The circle of white ash widens around it.
I get up and walk off in the moonlight and each time
I look back the red is deeper and the light smaller.
Scorpio rises late with Mars caught in his claw;
The moon has come before them, the light
Like a choir of children in the young laurel trees.
It is April; the shad, the hot headed fish,
Climbs the rivers; there is trillium in the damp canyons;
The foetid adder's tongue lolls by the waterfall.
There was a farm at this campsite once, it is almost gone now.
There were sheep here after the farm, and fire
Long ago burned the redwoods out of the gulch,
The Douglas fir off the ridge; today the soil

Is stony and incoherent, the small stones lie flat
And plate the surface like scales.
Twenty years ago the spreading gully
Toppled the big oak over onto the house.
Now there is nothing left but the foundations
Hidden in poison oak, and above on the ridge,
Six lonely, ominous fenceposts;
The redwood beams of the barn make a footbridge
Over the deep waterless creek bed;
The hills are covered with wild oats
Dry and white by midsummer.
I walk in the random survivals of the orchard.
In a patch of moonlight a mole
Shakes his tunnel like an angry vein;
Orion walks waist deep in the fog coming in from the ocean;
Leo crouches under the zenith.
There are tiny hard fruits already on the plum trees.
The purity of the apple blossoms is incredible.
As the wind dies down their fragrance
Clusters around them like thick smoke.
All the day they roared with bees, in the moonlight
They are silent and immaculate.

SPRING, SIERRA NEVADA

Once more golden Scorpio glows over the col
Above Deadman Canyon, orderly and brilliant,
Like an inspiration in the brain of Archimedes.
I have seen its light over the warm sea,
Over the coconut beaches, phosphorescent and pulsing;
And the living light in the water
Shivering away from the swimming hand,
Creeping against the lips, filling the floating hair.
Here where the glaciers have been and the snow stays late,
The stone is clean as light, the light steady as stone.
The relationship of stone, ice and stars is systematic and enduring
Novelty emerges after centuries, a rock spalls from the cliffs,
The glacier contracts and turns grayer,
The stream cuts new sinuosities in the meadow,
The sun moves through space and the earth with it,

The stars change places.
                    The snow has lasted longer this year,
Than anyone can remember. The lowest meadow is a lake,
The next two are snowfields, the pass is covered with snow,
Only the steepest rocks are bare. Between the pass
And the last meadow the snowfield gapes for a hundred feet,
In a narrow blue chasm through which a waterfall drops,
Spangled with sunset at the top, black and muscular
Where it disappears again in the snow.
The world is filled with hidden running water
That pounds in the ears like ether;
The granite needles rise from the snow, pale as steel;
Above the copper mine the cliff is blood red,
The white snow breaks at the edge of it;
The sky comes close to my eyes like the blue eyes
Of someone kissed in sleep.
                    I descend to camp,
To the young, sticky, wrinkled aspen leaves,
To the first violets and wild cyclamen,
And cook supper in the blue twilight.
All night deer pass over the snow on sharp hooves,
In the darkness their cold muzzles find the new grass
At the edge of the snow.

FALL, SIERRA NEVADA

This morning the hermit thrush was absent at breakfast,
His place was taken by a family of chickadees;
At noon a flock of humming birds passed south,
Whirling in the wind up over the saddle between
Ritter and Banner, following the migration lane
Of the Sierra crest southward to Guatemala.
All day cloud shadows have moved over the face of the mountain,
The shadow of a golden eagle weaving between them
Over the face of the glacier.
At sunset the half-moon rides on the bent back of the Scorpion,
The Great Bear kneels on the mountain.
Ten degrees below the moon
Venus sets in the haze arising from the Great Valley.
Jupiter, in opposition to the sun, rises in the alpenglow

There are rocks on the earth
And one who sleepless
Throbbed with the ten
Nightingales in the plum trees
Sleepless as Boötes stood over him
Gnawing the pillow
Sitting on the bed's edge smoking
Sitting by the window looking
One who rose in the false
Dawn and stoned
The nightingales in the garden
The heart pawned for wisdom
The heart
Bartered for knowledge and folly
The will troubled
The mind secretly aghast
The eyes and lips full of sorrow
The apices of vision wavering
As the flower spray at the tip of the windstalk
The becalmed sail
The heavy wordless weight
And now
The anguishing and pitiless file
Cutting away life
Capsule by capsule biting
Into the heart
The coal of fire
Sealing the lips
There are rocks on earth

And

In the Japanese quarter
A phonograph playing
"Moonlight on ruined castles"
Kojo n'suki
And
The movement of the wind fish
Keeping time to the music
Sirius setting behind it

(The Dog has scented the sun)
Gold immense fish
Squirm in the trade wind
"Young Middle Western woman
In rut
Desires correspondent"
The first bright flower
Cynoglossum
The blue hound's tongue
Breaks on the hill
"The tide has gone down
Over the reef
I walk about the world
There is great
Wind and then rain"
"My life is bought and paid for
So much pleasure
For so much pain"
The folded fossiliferous
Sedimentary rocks end here
The granite batholith
Obtrudes abruptly
West of the fault line
Betelgeuse reddens
Drawing its substance about it
It is possible that a process is beginning
Similar to that which lifted
The great Sierra fault block
Through an older metamorphic range

(The Dog barks on the sun's spoor)

Now
The thought of death
Binds fast the flood of light
Ten years ago the snow falling
All a long winter night
I had lain waking in my bed alone
Turning my heavy thoughts
And no way might
Sleep

Remembering divers things long gone
Now
In the long day in the hour of small shadow
I walk on the continent's last western hill
And lie prone among the iris in the grass
My eyes fixed on the durable stone
That speaks and hears as though it were myself

from THE PHOENIX AND THE TORTOISE
(1944)

I

Webs of misery spread in the brain,
In the dry Spring in the soft heat.
Dirty cotton bolls of cloud hang
At the sky's edge; vague yellow stratus
Glimmer behind them. It is storming
Somewhere far out in the ocean.
All night vast rollers exploded
Offshore; now the sea has subsided
To a massive, uneasy torpor.
Fragments of its inexhaustible
Life litter the shingle, sea hares,
Broken starfish, a dead octopus,
And everywhere, swarming like ants,
Innumerable hermit crabs,
Hungry and efficient as maggots.

This is not the first time this shingle
Has been here. These cobbles are washed
From ancient conglomerate beds,
Beaches of the Franciscan series,
The immense layer cake of grey strata
That hangs without top or bottom
In the geological past
Of the California Coast Ranges.
There are no fossils in them. Their
Dates are disputed—thousands of feet,
Thousands and thousands of years, of bays,
Tidemarshes, estuaries, beaches,
Where time flowed eventless as silt.
Further along the beach the stones
Change; the cliffs are yellow with black
Bands of lignite; and scattered amongst
The sand dollars in the storm's refuse

Are fossil sand dollars the sea
Has washed from stone, as it has washed
These, newly dead, from life.

                    And I,
Walking by the viscid, menacing
Water, turn with my heavy heart
In my baffled brain, Plutarch's page—
The falling light of the Spartan
Heroes in the late Hellenic dusk—
Agis, Cleomenes—this poem
Of the phoenix and the tortoise—
Of what survives and what perishes,
And how, of the fall of history
And waste of fact—on the crumbling
Edge of a ruined polity
That washes away in an ocean
Whose shores are all washing into death.

A group of terrified children
Has just discovered the body
Of a Japanese sailor bumping
In a snarl of kelp in a tidepool.
While the crowd collects, I stand, mute
As he, watching his smashed ribs breathe
Of the life of the ocean, his white
Torn bowels braid themselves with the kelp;
And, out of his drained grey flesh, he
Watches me with open hard eyes
Like small indestructible animals—
Me—who stand here on the edge of death,
Seeking the continuity,
The germ plasm, of history,
The epic's lyric absolute.

What happened, and what is remembered—
Or—history is the description
Of those forms of man's activity
Where value survives at the lowest
Level necessary to insure

Temporal continuity.
Or "as the Philosopher says,"
The historian differs from
The poet in this: the historian
Presents what did happen, the poet,
What might happen. For this reason
Poetry is more philosophic
Than history, and less trivial.
Poetry presents generalities,
History merely particulars.
So action is generalized
Into what an essential person
Must do by virtue of his essence—
Acting in an imaginary
Order of being, where existence
And essence, as in the Deity
Of Aquinas, fuse in pure act.
What happens in the mere occasion
To human beings is recorded
As an occurrence in the gulf
Between essence and existence—
An event of marginal content.

. . . .

II

I am cold in my folded blanket,
Huddled on the ground in the moonlight.

The crickets cry in congealing frost;
Field mice run over my body;
The frost thickens and the night goes by.

North of us lies the vindictive
Foolish city asleep under its guns;
Its rodent ambitions washing out
In sewage and unwholesome dreams.
Behind the backs of drowsy sentries

The moonlight shines through frosted glass—
On the floors of innumerable
Corridors the mystic symbols
Of the bureaucrats are reversed—
Mirrorwise, as Leonardo
Kept the fever charts of one person.
Two Ptahs, two Muhammad's coffins,
We float in the illimitable
Surgery of moonlight, isolate
From each other and the turning earth;
Motionless; frost on our faces;
Eyes by turns alive, dark in the dark.

The State is the organization
Of the evil instincts of mankind.
History is the penalty
We pay for original sin.
In the conflict of appetite
And desire, the person finally
Loses; either the technology
Of the choice of the lesser evil
Overwhelms him; or a universe
Where the stars in their courses move
To ends that justify their means
Dissolves him in its elements.
He cannot win, not on this table.
The World, the Flesh, and the Devil—
The Tempter offered Christ mastery
Of the three master institutions,
Godparents of all destruction—
"Miracle, Mystery, and Authority—"
The systematization of
Appetitive choice to obtain
Desire by accumulation.

History continuously
Bleeds to death through a million secret
Wounds of trivial hunger and fear.
Its stockholders' private disasters
Are amortized in catastrophe.

War is the health of the State? Indeed!
War is the State. All personal
Anti-institutional values
Must be burnt out of each generation.
If a massive continuum
Of personality endured
Into grandchildren, history
Would stop.

IV

Dark within dark I cling to sleep,
The heart's capsule closed in the fist
Of circumstance; prison within
Prison, inseparably dark,
I struggle to hold oblivion
As Jacob struggled in a dream,
And woke touched and with another name.
And on the thin brainpan of sleep
The mill of Gaza grinds;
The heart condenses; and beyond
The world's lip the sun to me is dark
And silent as the moon that falls
Through the last degrees of night into
The unknown antipodes. I lie
At random, carelessly diffused,
Stone and amoeba on the verge
Of partition; and beyond the reach
Of my drowsy integrity,
The race of glory and the race
Of shame, just or unjust, alike
Miserable, both come to evil end.

Eventually history
Distills off all accumulated
Values but one. Babies are more
Durable than monuments, the rose
Outlives Ausonius, Ronsard,

And Waller, and Horace's pear tree
His immortal column. Once more
Process is precipitated
In the tirelessly receptive womb.
In the decay of the sufficient
Reasonableness of sacraments
Marriage holds by its bona fides.

Beneath what shield and from what flame.

The darkness gathers about Lawrence
Dying by the dead Mediterranean—
Catullus is psychoanalyzed
Between wars in lickerish London.
Another aging précieux
Drinks cognac, dreams of rutting children
In the Mississippi Valley,
Watches the Will destroy the logic
Of Christopher Wren and Richelieu.
Schweitzer plays Bach in the jungle.
It is all over—just and unjust.
The seed leaks through the gravel.

The light grows stronger and my lids
That were black turn red; the blood turns
To the coming sun. I sit up
And look out over the bright quiet
Sea and the blue and yellow cliffs
And the pure white tatters of fog
Dissolving on the black fir ridges.
The world is immovable
And immaculate. The argument
Has come to an end; it is morning,
And in the isolating morning
The problem hangs suspended, lucid
In a crystal cabinet of air
And angels where only bird song wakes.

"Value is the elastic ether
Of quality that fills up the gaps

In the continuum of discreet
Quality—the prime togetherness."
The assumption of order,
The principle of parsimony,
Remain mysteries; fact and logic
Meet only in catastrophe.
So long ago they discovered that
Each new irrational is the start
Of a new series of numbers;
Called God the source of systematic
Irrationalization of given
Order—the organism that
Geometricizes. And that vain
Boy, systematically deranging
Himself amongst the smoky cannoneers
Of the Commune, finding a bronze
Apotheosis as the perfect
Provincial French merchant who made good.
The statistical likelihood
Of being blown to pieces.

"Value is the reflection
Of satisfied appetite."
The State organizes ecstasy.
The dinosaur wallows in the chilling
Marsh. The bombs fall on the packed dance halls.
The sperm seeks the egg in the gravel.
"Novelty is, by definition,
Value-positive."

                "Value
Is a phase change in the relations
Of events." Does that mean anything?

Morning. It is Good Friday Morning;
Communion has past to Agony
And Agony is gone and only
Responsibility remains; doom
Watches with its inorganic eyes,

The bright, blind regiments, hidden
By the sun-flushed sky, the remote
Indestructible animals.

Value, causality, being,
Are reducible to the purest
Act, the self-determining person,
He who discriminates structure
In contingency, he who assumes
All the responsibility
Of ordered, focused, potential—
Sustained by all the universe,
Focusing the universe in act—
The person, the absolute price,
The only blood defiance of doom.

Whymper, coming down the Matterhorn,
After the mountain had collected
Its terrible, casual fee,
The blackmail of an imbecile beauty:
"About 6 PM we arrived
Upon the ridge descending towards
Zermatt, and all peril was over.
We frequently looked, but in vain,
For traces of our unfortunate
Companions; we bent over the ridge
And cried to them, but no sound returned.
Convinced at last that they were neither
Within sight nor hearing we ceased;
And, too cast down for speech, silently
Gathered up our things and the little
Effects of those who were lost
And prepared to continue
The descent. When, lo! a mighty arch
And beneath it a huge cross of light
Appeared, rising above the Lyskamm
High into the sky. Pale, colorless,
And noiseless, but perfectly sharp
And defined, except where it was lost
In the clouds, this unearthly

Apparition seemed like a vision
From another world; and appalled,
We watched with amazement the gradual
Development of two vast crosses
One on either side . . . Our movements
Had no effect on it, the spectral
Forms remained motionless. It was
A fearful and wonderful sight;
Unique in my experience,
And impressive beyond description,
Coming at such a moment."

Nude, my feet in the cold shallows,
The motion of the water surface
Barely perceptible, and the sand
Of the bottom in fine sharp ridges
Under my toes, I wade out, waist deep
And swim seaward down the narrow inlet.
In the distance, beyond the sand bar,
The combers are breaking, and nearer,
Like a wave crest escaped and frozen,
One white egret guards the harbor mouth.
The immense stellar phenomenon
Of dawn focuses in the egret
And flows out, and focuses in me
And flows infinitely away
To touch the last galactic dust.

This is the prime reality—
Bird and man, the individual
Discriminate, the self evalued
Actual, the operation
Of infinite, ordered potential.
Birds, sand grains, and souls bleed into being;
The past reclaims its own, "I should have,
I could have—It might have been different—"
Sunsets on Saturn, desert roses,
Corruptions of the will, quality—

The determinable future, fall
Into quantity, into the
Irreparable past, history's
Cruel irresponsibility.

This is the minimum negative
Condition, the "Condition humaine,"
The tragic loss of value into
Barren novelty, the condition
Of salvation; out of this alone
The person emerges as complete
Responsible act—this lost
And that conserved—the appalling
Decision of the verb "to be."
Men drop dead in the ancient rubbish
Of the Acropolis, scholars fall
Into self-dug graves, Jews are smashed
Like heroic vermin in the Polish winter.
This is my fault, the horrible term
Of weakness, evasion, indulgence,
The total of my petty fault—
No other man's.

           And out of this
Shall I reclaim beauty, peace of soul,
The perfect gift of self-sacrifice,
Myself as act, as immortal person?

I walk back along the sandspit,
The horizon cuts the moon in half,
And far out at sea a path of light,
Violent and brilliant, reflected
From high stratus clouds and then again
On the moving sea, the invisible
Sunrise spreads its light before the moon.

My wife has been swimming in the breakers,
She comes up the beach to meet me, nude,
Sparkling with water, singing high and clear
Against the surf. The sun crosses

The hills and fills her hair, as it lights
The moon and glorifies the sea
And deep in the empty mountains melts
The snow of Winter and the glaciers
Of ten thousand thousand years.

WHEN WE WITH SAPPHO

". . . about the cool water
the wind sounds through sprays
of apple, and from the quivering leaves
slumber pours down . . ."

We lie here in the bee filled, ruinous
Orchard of a decayed New England farm,
Summer in our hair, and the smell
Of summer in our twined bodies,
Summer in our mouths, and summer
In the luminous, fragmentary words
Of this dead Greek woman.
Stop reading. Lean back. Give me your mouth.
Your grace is as beautiful as sleep.
You move against me like a wave
That moves in sleep.
Your body spreads across my brain
Like a bird filled summer;
Not like a body, not like a separate thing,
But like a nimbus that hovers
Over every other thing in all the world.
Lean back. You are beautiful,
As beautiful as the folding
Of your hands in sleep.

We have grown old in the afternoon.
Here in our orchard we are as old
As she is now, wherever dissipate
In that distant sea her gleaming dust
Flashes in the wave crest

Or stains the murex shell.
All about us the old farm subsides
Into the honey bearing chaos of high summer.
In those far islands the temples
Have fallen away, and the marble
Is the color of wild honey.
There is nothing left of the gardens
That were once about them, of the fat
Turf marked with cloven hooves.
Only the sea grass struggles
Over the crumbled stone,
Over the splintered steps,
Only the blue and yellow
Of the sea, and the cliffs
Red in the distance across the bay.
Lean back.
Her memory has passed to our lips now.
Our kisses fall through summer's chaos
In our own breasts and thighs.

Gold colossal domes of cumulus cloud
Lift over the undulant, sibilant forest.
The air presses against the earth.
Thunder breaks over the mountains.
Far off, over the Adirondacks,
Lightning quivers, almost invisible
In the bright sky, violet against
The grey, deep shadows of the bellied clouds.
The sweet virile hair of thunder storms
Brushes over the swelling horizon.
Take off your shoes and stockings.
I will kiss your sweet legs and feet
As they lie half buried in the tangle
Of rank scented midsummer flowers.
Take off your clothes. I will press
Your summer honeyed flesh into the hot
Soil, into the crushed, acrid herbage
Of midsummer. Let your body sink
Like honey through the hot
Granular fingers of summer.

Rest. Wait. We have enough for a while.
Kiss me with your mouth
Wet and ragged, your mouth that tastes
Of my own flesh. Read to me again
The twisting music of that language
That is of all others, itself a work of art.
Read again those isolate, poignant words
Saved by ancient grammarians
To illustrate the conjugations
And declensions of the more ancient dead.
Lean back in the curve of my body,
Press your bruised shoulders against
The damp hair of my body.
Kiss me again. Think, sweet linguist,
In this world the ablative is impossible.
No other one will help us here.
We must help ourselves to each other.
The wind walks slowly away from the storm;
Veers on the wooded crests; sounds
In the valleys. Here we are isolate,
One with the other; and beyond
This orchard lies isolation,
The isolation of all the world.
Never let anything intrude
On the isolation of this day,
These words, isolate on dead tongues,
This orchard, hidden from fact and history,
These shadows, blended in the summer light,
Together isolate beyond the world's reciprocity.

Do not talk any more. Do not speak.
Do not break silence until
We are weary of each other.
Let our fingers run like steel
Carving the contours of our bodies' gold.
Do not speak. My face sinks
In the clotted summer of your hair.
The sound of the bees stops.
Stillness falls like a cloud.
Be still. Let your body fall away

Into the awe filled silence
Of the fulfilled summer—
Back, back, infinitely away—
Our lips weak, faint with stillness.

See. The sun has fallen away.
Now there are amber
Long lights on the shattered
Boles of the ancient apple trees.
Our bodies move to each other
As bodies move in sleep;
At once filled and exhausted,
As the summer moves to autumn,
As we, with Sappho, move towards death.
My eyelids sink toward sleep in the hot
Autumn of your uncoiled hair.
Your body moves in my arms
On the verge of sleep;
And it is as though I held
In my arms the bird filled
Evening sky of summer.

LUTE MUSIC

The earth will be going on a long time
Before it finally freezes;
Men will be on it; they will take names,
Give their deeds reasons.
We will be here only
As chemical constituents—
A small franchise indeed.
Right now we have lives,
Corpuscles, ambitions, caresses,
Like everybody had once—
All the bright neige d'antan people,
"Blithe Helen, white Iope, and the rest,"
All the uneasy, remembered dead.

Here at the year's end, at the feast
Of birth, let us bring to each other
The gifts brought once west through deserts—
The precious metal of our mingled hair,
The frankincense of enraptured arms and legs,
The myrrh of desperate, invincible kisses—
Let us celebrate the daily
Recurrent nativity of love,
The endless epiphany of our fluent selves,
While the earth rolls away under us
Into unknown snows and summers,
Into untraveled spaces of the stars.

FLOATING

Our canoe idles in the idling current
Of the tree and vine and rush enclosed
Backwater of a torpid midwestern stream;
Revolves slowly, and lodges in the glutted
Waterlilies. We are tired of paddling.
All afternoon we have climbed the weak current,
Up dim meanders, through woods and pastures,
Past muddy fords where the strong smell of cattle
Lay thick across the water; singing the songs
Of perfect, habitual motion; ski songs,
Nightherding songs, songs of the capstan walk,
The levee, and the roll of the voyageurs.
Tired of motion, of the rhythms of motion,
Tired of the sweet play of our interwoven strength,
We lie in each other's arms and let the palps
Of waterlily leaf and petal hold back
All motion in the heat thickened, drowsing air.
Sing to me softly, Westron Wynde, Ah the Syghes,
Mon coeur se recommend à vous, Phoebi Claro;
Sing the wandering erotic melodies
Of men and women gone seven hundred years,
Softly, your mouth close to my cheek.
Let our thighs lie entangled on the cushions,

Let your breasts in their thin cover
Hang pendant against my naked arms and throat;
Let your odorous hair fall across our eyes;
Kiss me with those subtle, melodic lips.
As I undress you, your pupils are black, wet,
Immense, and your skin ivory and humid.
Move softly, move hardly at all, part your thighs,
Take me slowly while our gnawing lips
Fumble against the humming blood in our throats.
Move softly, do not move at all, but hold me,
Deep, still, deep within you, while time slides away,
As this river slides beyond this lily bed,
And the thieving moments fuse and disappear
In our mortal, timeless flesh.

ANOTHER SPRING

The seasons revolve and the years change
With no assistance or supervision.
The moon, without taking thought,
Moves in its cycle, full, crescent, and full.

The white moon enters the heart of the river;
The air is drugged with azalea blossoms;
Deep in the night a pine cone falls;
Our campfire dies out in the empty mountains.

The sharp stars flicker in the tremulous branches;
The lake is black, bottomless in the crystalline night;
High in the sky the Northern Crown
Is cut in half by the dim summit of a snow peak.

O heart, heart, so singularly
Intransigent and corruptible,
Here we lie entranced by the starlit water,
And moments that should each last forever

Slide unconsciously by us like water.

THE ADVANTAGES OF LEARNING

I am a man with no ambitions
And few friends, wholly incapable
Of making a living, growing no
Younger, fugitive from some just doom.
Lonely, ill-clothed, what does it matter?
At midnight I make myself a jug
Of hot white wine and cardamon seeds.
In a torn grey robe and old beret,
I sit in the cold writing poems,
Drawing nudes on the crooked margins,
Copulating with sixteen year old
Nymphomaniacs of my imagination.

INVERSELY, AS THE SQUARE OF
THEIR DISTANCES APART

It is impossible to see anything
In this dark; but I know this is me, Rexroth,
Plunging through the night on a chilling planet.
It is warm and busy in this vegetable
Darkness where invisible deer feed quietly.
The sky is warm and heavy, even the trees
Over my head cannot be distinguished,
But I know they are knobcone pines, that their cones
Endure unopened on the branches, at last
To grow imbedded in the wood, waiting for fire
To open them and reseed the burned forest.
And I am waiting, alone, in the mountains,
In the forest, in the darkness, and the world
Falls swiftly on its measured ellipse.

It is warm tonight and very still.
The stars are hazy and the river—
Vague and monstrous under the fireflies—
Is hardly audible, resonant
And profound at the edge of hearing.
I can just see your eyes and wet lips.
Invisible, solemn, and fragrant,
Your flesh opens to me in secret.
We shall know no further enigma.
After all the years there is nothing
Stranger than this. We who know ourselves
As one doubled thing, and move our limbs
As deft implements of one fused lust,
Are mysteries in each other's arms.

At the wood's edge in the moonlight
We dropped our clothes and stood naked,
Swaying, shadow mottled, enclosed
In each other and together
Closed in the night. We did not hear
The whip-poor-will, nor the aspen's
Whisper; the owl flew silently
Or cried out loud, we did not know.
We could not hear beyond the heart.
We could not see the moving dark
And light, the stars that stood or moved,
The stars that fell. Did they all fall
We had not known. We were falling
Like meteors, dark through black cold
Toward each other, and then compact,
Blazing through air into the earth.

I lie alone in an alien
Bed in a strange house and morning

More cruel than any midnight
Pours its brightness through the window—
Cherry branches with the flowers
Fading, and behind them the gold
Stately baubles of the maple,
And behind them the pure immense
April sky and a white frayed cloud,
And in and behind everything,
The inescapable vacant
Distance of loneliness.

BETWEEN TWO WARS

Remember that breakfast one November—
Cold black grapes smelling faintly
Of the cork they were packed in,
Hard rolls with hot, white flesh,
And thick, honey sweetened chocolate?
And the parties at night; the gin and the tangos?
The torn hair nets, the lost cuff links?
Where have they all gone to,
The beautiful girls, the abandoned hours?
They said we were lost, mad and immoral,
And interfered with the plans of the management.
And today, millions and millions, shut alive
In the coffins of circumstance,
Beat on the buried lids,
Huddle in the cellars of ruins, and quarrel
Over their own fragmented flesh.

DELIA REXROTH

Died June, 1916

Under your illkempt yellow roses,
Delia, today you are younger
Than your son. Two and a half decades—

The family monument sagged askew,
And he overtook your half-a-life.
On the other side of the country,
Near the willows by the slow river,
Deep in the earth, the white ribs retain
The curve of your fervent, careful breast;
The fine skull, the ardor of your brain.
And in the fingers the memory
Of Chopin études, and in the feet
Slow waltzes and champagne twosteps sleep.
And the white full moon of midsummer,
That you watched awake all that last night,
Watches history fill the deserts
And oceans with corpses once again;
And looks in the east window at me,
As I move past you to middle age
And knowledge past your agony and waste.

ANDREE REXROTH

Died October, 1940

Now once more gray mottled buckeye branches
Explode their emerald stars,
And alders smoulder in a rosy smoke
Of innumerable buds.
I know that spring again is splendid
As ever, the hidden thrush
As sweetly tongued, the sun as vital—
But these are the forest trails we walked together,
These paths, ten years together.
We thought the years would last forever,
They are all gone now, the days
We thought would not come for us are here.
Bright trout poised in the current—
The raccoon's track at the water's edge—
A bittern booming in the distance—
Your ashes scattered on this mountain—
Moving seaward on this stream.

from THE ART OF WORDLY WISDOM (1949)

THE THIN EDGE OF YOUR PRIDE

1922-1926

Poems for Leslie Smith

I

Later when the gloated water
Burst with red lotus; when perfect green
Enameled grass and tree, "I most solitary,
Boating," rested thoughtful on the moated water;
Where the low sun spread crimson
Interstices in the glowing lotus; aware
Of the coming, deep in the years, of a time
When these lagoons and darkening trees,
This twilight sliding mirror where we have floated,
Would surge hugely out of memory
Into some distant, ordinary evening—
Hugely, in vertigo and awe.

II

Six months as timeless as dream,
As impotent . . .
You pause on the subway stairs,
Wave and smile and descend.
Was it an instant between waking
And waking,
That you smile and wave again,
Two blocks away on a smoky
Chicago boulevard?
How many dynasties decayed
Meanwhile, how many
Times did the second hand
Circumvent its dial?

III

Indigenes of furnished rooms,
Our best hours have been passed
At the taxpayers' expense
In the public parks of four cities.
It could be worse, the level
Well-nurtured lawns, the uplifted
Rhythmic arms of children,
A bright red ball following
A graph of laughter,
The dresses of the little girls
Blossoming like hyacinths
In early August, the fountains,
The tame squirrels, pigeons
And sparrows, and other
Infinitely memorable things.

IV

Chill and abandoned, the pavilion
In Jackson Park stands like a sightless
Lighthouse beside the lake.
It is very dark, there would be no moon
Even if the night were not thickly overcast.
The wind moans in the rustic carpentry,
But the rain returns silently to the water,
Without even a hiss or a whisper.
We have the shadows to ourselves,
The lovers, the psychopathic, the lonely,
Have gone indoors for the winter.
We have been here in other autumns,
Nights when the wind stirred this inland water
Like the sea, piled the waves over the breakwater,
And onto the highway, tore apart tall clouds,
And revealed the moon, rushing dead white
Over the city.

V

The absorbent, glimmering night
Receives a solitary nighthawk cry;
Marshalls its naked housefronts;
And waits.
The lights of a passing yacht
Jewel for a moment your windblown hair.
The shadows of the lombardy poplars
Tilt like planks on water.
The sea breeze smells faintly of hospitals.
Far off,
On the desert coasts of the Antipodes,
Mountains slide silently into the sea.

VI

Paradise Pond

The minute fingers of the imperceptible air
Arrange a shadow tracery of leaf and hair
About your face.
Downstream a group of Hungarians from the mill,
Stiff with unaccustomed ease,
Catch insignificant fish.
A row of brown ducklings jerks itself across the water,
Moving like furry cartridges
Into some beneficent machine gun.
We shall arise presently, having said nothing,
And hand in vibrating hand walk back the way we came.

VII

I think these squalid houses are the ghosts
Of dinosaur and mammoth and all
The other giants now long rotted from the earth.
I think that on lonely nights when we,
Disparate, distraught, half a continent between us,
Walk the deserted streets,
They take their ancient forms again,
And shift and move ahead of us
For elbow room; and as we pass

They touch us here and there,
Softly, awestruck, curious;
And then with lurching step
Close in upon our heels.

VIII

"Whether or not, it is no question now,
Of time or place, or even how,
It is not time for questions now,
Nor yet the place."
The soft lights of your face
Arrange themselves in memories
Of smiles and frowns.
You are reading,
Propped up in the window seat;
And I stand hesitant at the rug's edge . . .
Whether or not . . . it is no question now.
I wonder what we have done
To merit such ironic lives.
Hesitant on the rug's edge,
I study the kaleidoscope
Before my toes, where some long
Dead Persian has woven
A cynical, Levantine prayer.

IX

After an hour the mild
Confusion of snow
Amongst the lamplights
Has softened and subdued
The nervous lines of bare
Branches etched against
The chill twilight.
Now behind me, upon the pallid
Expanse of empty boulevard,
The snow reclaims from the darkened
Staring shop windows,
One by one, a single
Line of footprints.

X

Out of the westborne snow shall come a memory
Floated upon it by my hands,
By my lips that remember your kisses.
It shall caress your hands, your lips,
Your breasts, your thighs, with kisses,
As real as flesh, as real as memory of flesh.
I shall come to you with the spring,
Spring's flesh in the world,
Translucent narcissus, dogwood like a vision,
And phallic crocus,
Spring's flesh in my hands.

XI

Someone has cast an unwary match
Into the litter of the tamarack woodlot.
A herd of silent swine watch the long flames
Blend into the sunset.
By midnight the fire is cold,
But long streamers of grey smoke
Still drift between the blackened trees,
And mingle with the mist and fireflies
Of the marsh.
I shall not sleep well tonight.
Tomorrow three days will have passed
Since I have heard your voice.

XII

After a hundred years have slept above us
Autumn will still be painting the Berkshires;
Gold and purple storms will still
Climb over the Catskills.
They will have to look a long time
For my name in the musty corners of libraries;
Utter forgetfulness will mock
Your uncertain ambitions.
But there will be other lovers,
Walking along the hill crests,

Climbing, to sit entranced
On pinnacles in the sunset,
In the moonrise.
The Catskills,
The Berkshires,
Have good memories.

XIII

This shall be sufficient,
A few black buildings against the dark dawn,
The bands of blue lightless streets,
The air splotched with the gold,
Electric, coming day.

XIV

You alone,
A white robe over your naked body,
Passing and repassing
Through the dreams of twenty years.

BETWEEN MYSELF AND DEATH

To Jimmy Blanton's Music:
Sophisticated Lady, Body and Soul

A fervor parches you sometimes,
And you hunch over it, silent,
Cruel, and timid; and sometimes
You are frightened with wantonness,
And give me your desperation.
Mostly we lurk in our coverts,
Protecting our spleens, pretending
That our bandages are our wounds.
But sometimes the wheel of change stops;
Illusion vanishes in peace;
And suddenly pride lights your flesh—
Lucid as diamond, wise as pearl—
And your face, remote, absolute,
Perfect and final like a beast's.
It is wonderful to watch you,
A living woman in a room
Full of frantic, sterile people,
And think of your arching buttocks
Under your velvet evening dress,
And the beautiful fire spreading
From your sex, burning flesh and bone,
The unbelievably complex
Tissues of your brain all alive
Under your coiling, splendid hair.

I like to think of you naked.
I put your naked body
Between myself alone and death.

If I go into my brain
And set fire to your sweet nipples,
To the tendons beneath your knees,
I can see far before me.
It is empty there where I look,
But at least it is lighted.

I know how your shoulders glisten,
How your face sinks into trance,
And your eyes like a sleepwalker's,
And your lips of a woman
Cruel to herself.
                    I like to
Think of you clothed, your body
Shut to the world and self contained,
Its wonderful arrogance
That makes all women envy you.
I can remember every dress,
Each more proud then a naked nun.
When I go to sleep my eyes
Close in a mesh of memory.
Its cloud of intimate odor
Dreams instead of myself.

THE SIGNATURE OF ALL THINGS

My head and shoulders, and my book
In the cool shade, and my body
Stretched bathing in the sun, I lie
Reading beside the waterfall—
Boehme's "Signature of all Things."
Through the deep July day the leaves
Of the laurel, all the colors
Of gold, spin down through the moving
Deep laurel shade all day. They float
On the mirrored sky and forest
For a while, and then, still slowly

Spinning, sink through the crystal deep
Of the pool to its leaf gold floor.
The saint saw the world as streaming
In the electrolysis of love.
I put him by and gaze through shade
Folded into shade of slender
Laurel trunks and leaves filled with sun.
The wren broods in her moss domed nest.
A newt struggles with a white moth
Drowning in the pool. The hawks scream,
Playing together on the ceiling
Of heaven. The long hours go by.
I think of those who have loved me,
Of all the mountains I have climbed,
Of all the seas I have swum in.
The evil of the world sinks.
My own sin and trouble fall away
Like Christian's bundle, and I watch
My forty summers fall like falling
Leaves and falling water held
Eternally in summer air.

———————

Deer are stamping in the glades,
Under the full July moon.
There is a smell of dry grass
In the air, and more faintly,
The scent of a far off skunk.
As I stand at the wood's edge,
Watching the darkness, listening
To the stillness, a small owl
Comes to the branch above me,
On wings more still than my breath.
When I turn my light on him,
His eyes glow like drops of iron,
And he perks his head at me,
Like a curious kitten.
The meadow is bright as snow.

My dog prowls the grass, a dark
Blur in the blur of brightness.
I walk to the oak grove where
The Indian village was once.
There, in blotched and cobwebbed light
And dark, dim in the blue haze,
Are twenty Holstein heifers,
Black and white, all lying down,
Quietly together, under
The huge trees rooted in the graves.

———————

When I dragged the rotten log
From the bottom of the pool,
It seemed heavy as stone.
I let it lie in the sun
For a month; and then chopped it
Into sections, and split them
For kindling, and spread them out
To dry some more. Late that night,
After reading for hours,
While moths rattled at the lamp—
The saints and the philosophers
On the destiny of man—
I went out on my cabin porch,
And looked up through the black forest
At the swaying islands of stars.
Suddenly I saw at my feet,
Spread on the floor of night, ingots
Of quivering phosphorescence,
And all about were scattered chips
Of pale cold light that was alive.

LYELL'S HYPOTHESIS AGAIN

*An Attempt to Explain the Former
Changes of the Earth's Surface by
Causes Now in Operation*
Subtitle of Lyell: Principles of Geology

The mountain road ends here,
Broken away in the chasm where
The bridge washed out years ago.
The first scarlet larkspur glitters
In the first patch of April
Morning sunlight. The engorged creek
Roars and rustles like a military
Ball. Here by the waterfall,
Insuperable life, flushed
With the equinox, sentient
And sentimental, falls away
To the sea and death. The tissue
Of sympathy and agony
That binds the flesh in its Nessus' shirt;
The clotted cobweb of unself
And self; sheds itself and flecks
The sun's bed with darts of blossom
Like flagellant blood above
The water bursting in the vibrant
Air. This ego, bound by personal
Tragedy and the vast
Impersonal vindictiveness
Of the ruined and ruining world,
Pauses in this immortality,
As passionate, as apathetic,
As the lava flow that burned here once;
And stopped here; and said, 'This far
And no further.' And spoke thereafter
In the simple diction of stone.

Naked in the warm April air,
We lie under the redwoods,
In the sunny lee of a cliff.
As you kneel above me I see
Tiny red marks on your flanks
Like bites, where the redwood cones
Have pressed into your flesh.
You can find just the same marks
In the lignite in the cliff
Over our heads. *Sequoia
Langsdorfii* before the ice,
And *sempervirens* afterwards,
There is little difference,
Except for all those years.

Here in the sweet, moribund
Fetor of spring flowers, washed,
Flotsam and jetsam together,
Cool and naked together,
Under this tree for a moment,
We have escaped the bitterness
Of love, and love lost, and love
Betrayed. And what might have been,
And what might be, fall equally
Away with what is, and leave
Only these ideograms
Printed on the immortal
Hydrocarbons of flesh and stone.

DELIA REXROTH

California rolls into
Sleepy summer, and the air
Is full of the bitter sweet
Smoke of the grass fires burning
On the San Francisco hills.
Flesh burns so, and the pyramids

46

Likewise, and the burning stars.
Tired tonight, in a city
Of parvenus, in the inhuman
West, in the most blood drenched year,
I took down a book of poems
That you used to like, that you
Used to sing to music I
Never found anywhere again —
Michael Field's book, *Long Ago*.
Indeed it's long ago now —
Your bronze hair and svelte body.
I guess you were a fierce lover,
A wild wife, an animal
Mother. And now life has cost
Me more years, though much less pain,
Than you had to pay for it.
And I have bought back, for and from
Myself, these poems and paintings,
Carved from the protesting bone,
The precious consequences
Of your torn and distraught life.

ANDREE REXROTH

MT. TAMALPAIS

The years have gone. It is spring
Again. Mars and Saturn will
Soon come on, low in the West,
In the dusk. Now the evening
Sunlight makes hazy girders
Over Steep Ravine above
The waterfalls. The winter
Birds from Oregon, robins
And varied thrushes, feast on
Ripe toyon and madroñe
Berries. The robins sing as

The dense light falls.
                              Your ashes
Were scattered in this place. Here
I wrote you a farewell poem,
And long ago another,
A poem of peace and love,
Of the lassitude of a long
Spring evening in youth. Now
It is almost ten years since
You came here to stay. Once more,
The pussy willows that come
After the New Year in this
Outlandish land are blooming.
There are deer and raccoon tracks
In the same places. A few
New sand bars and cobble beds
Have been left where erosion
Has gnawed deep into the hills.
The rounds of life are narrow.
War and peace have past like ghosts.
The human race sinks towards
Oblivion. A bittern
Calls from the same rushes where
You heard one on our first year
In the West; and where I heard
One again in the year
Of your death.

KINGS RIVER CANYON

My sorrow is so wide
I cannot see across it;
And so deep I shall never
Reach the bottom of it.
The moon sinks through deep haze,
As though the Kings River Canyon
Were filled with fine, warm, damp gauze.
Saturn gleams through the thick light
Like a gold, wet eye; nearby,
Antares glows faintly,

Without sparkle. Far overhead,
Stone shines darkly in the moonlight —
Lookout Point, where we lay
In another full moon, and first
Peered down into this canyon.
Here we camped, by still autumnal
Pools, all one warm October.
I baked you a bannock birthday cake.
Here you did your best paintings —
Innocent, wondering landscapes.
Very few of them are left
Anywhere. You destroyed them
In the terrible trouble
Of your long sickness. Eighteen years
Have passed since that autumn.
There was no trail here then.
Only a few people knew
How to enter this canyon.
We were all alone, twenty
Miles from anybody;

A young husband and wife,
Closed in and wrapped about
In the quiet autumn,
In the sound of quiet water,
In the turning and falling leaves,
In the wavering of innumerable
Bats from the caves, dipping
Over the odorous pools
Where the great trout drowsed in the evenings.

Eighteen years have been ground
To pieces in the wheels of life.
You are dead. With a thousand
Convicts they have blown a highway
Through Horseshoe Bend. Youth is gone,
That only came once. My hair
Is turning grey and my body
Heavier. I too move on to death.
I think of Henry King's stilted

But desolated *Exequy*,
Of Yuan Chen's great poem,
Unbearably pitiful;
Alone by the Spring river
More alone than I had ever
Imagined I would ever be,
I think of Frieda Lawrence,
Sitting alone in New Mexico,
In the long drought, listening
For the hiss of the milky Isar,
Over the cobbles, in a lost Spring.

A LETTER TO
WILLIAM CARLOS WILLIAMS

Dear Bill,

When I search the past for you,
Sometimes I think you are like
St. Francis, whose flesh went out
Like a happy cloud from him,
And merged with every lover —
Donkeys, flowers, lepers, suns —
But I think you are more like
Brother Juniper, who suffered
All indignities and glories
Laughing like a gentle fool.
You're in the *Fioretti*
Somewhere, for you're a fool, Bill,
Like the Fool in Yeats, the term
Of all wisdom and beauty.
It's you, stands over against
Helen in all her wisdom,
Solomon in all his glory.

Remember years ago, when
I told you you were the first

Great Franciscan poet since
The Middle Ages? I disturbed
The even tenor of dinner.
Your wife thought I was crazy.
It's true, though. And you're 'pure', too,
A real classic, though not loud
About it—a whole lot like
The girls of the Anthology.
Not like strident Sappho, who
For all her grandeur, must have
Had endemetriosis,
But like Anyte, who says
Just enough, softly, for all
The thousands of years to remember.

It's a wonderful quiet
You have, a way of keeping
Still about the world, and its
Dirty rivers, and garbage cans,
Red wheelbarrows glazed with rain,
Cold plums stolen from the icebox,
And Queen Anne's lace, and day's eyes,
And leaf buds bursting over
Muddy roads, and splotched bellies
With babies in them, and Cortes
And Malinche on the bloody
Causeway, the death of the flower world.

Nowadays, when the press reels
With chatterboxes, you keep still,
Each year a sheaf of stillness,
Poems that have nothing to say,
Like the stillness of George Fox,
Sitting still under the cloud
Of all the world's temptation,
By the fire, in the kitchen,
In the Vale of Beavor. And
The archetype, the silence
Of Christ, when he paused a long
Time and then said, 'Thou sayest it'.

Now in a recent poem you say,
'I who am about to die.'
Maybe this is just a tag
From the classics, but it sends
A shudder over me. Where
Do you get that stuff, Williams?
Look at here. The day will come
When a young woman will walk
By the lucid Williams River,
Where it flows through an idyllic
News from Nowhere sort of landscape,
And she will say to her children,
'Isn't it beautiful? It
Is named after a man who
Walked here once when it was called
The Passaic, and was filthy
With the poisonous excrements
Of sick men and factories.
He was a great man. He knew
It was beautiful then, although
Nobody else did, back there
In the Dark Ages. And the
Beautiful river he saw
Still flows in his veins, as it
Does in ours, and flows in our eyes,
And flows in time, and makes us
Part of it, and part of him.
That, children, is what is called
A sacramental relationship.
And that is what a poet
Is, children, one who creates
Sacramental relationships
That last always.'
    With love and admiration,
    Kenneth Rexroth.

from THE DRAGON AND THE UNICORN
(1952)

I

"And what is love?" said Pilate,
And washed his hands.

All night long
The white snow falls on the white
Peaks through the quiet darkness.
The overland express train
Drives through the night, through the snow.
In the morning the land slopes
To the Atlantic, the sky
Is thicker, Spring stirs, smelling
Like old wet wood, new life speaks
In pale green fringes of marsh
Marigolds on the edges
Of the mountain snow drifts. Spring
Is only a faint green haze
On the high plains, only haze
And the fences that disappear
Over the horizon, and the
Rails, and the telegraph
Poles and the pale singing wires
Going on and on forever.

All things are made new by fire.
The plow in the furrow, Burns
Or Buddha, the first call to
Vocation, the severed worms,
The shattered mouse nest, the seed
Dripping from the bloody sword.
The sleepers chuckle under
The wheels, mocking the heartbeat.

We think of time as serial
And atomic, the expression
By mechanical means of a
Philosophical notion,
Regular divisibility
With a least common divisor
Of motion by motion, so
Many ticks to a century.
Such a thing does not exist.
Actually, the concept
Of time arose from the weaving
Together of the great organic
Cycles of the universe,
Sunrise and sunset, the moon
Waxing and waning, the changing
Stars and seasons, the climbing
And declining sun in heaven,
The round of sowing and harvest,
And the life and death of man.

The doom of versifying—
Orpheus was torn to pieces
By the vindictiveness of
Women or struck down by the
Jealousy of heaven.

The doom of the testicles—
Chiron's masculinity
Was so intense that all his
Children were adopted and
Later destroyed by the gods.

The deed done, Orestes draws
His steel penis like a snake
From its hole. The sun and moon
In Capricorn, Electra,
The little she goat, bleats and squirms,
Her brother between her thighs.
From whose wounds pour forth both blood
And water, the wine of whose

Maidenhead turns to water
Of baptism, the fiery
Mixture of being and not being.
The artist is his own mother.

Chicago, the train plunges through
A vast dome of electric gloom.
Cold wind, deepening dark, miles
Of railroad lights, 22nd
And Wentworth. The old Chinese
Restaurants now tourist joints.
Gooey Sam where we once roared
And taught the waiters to say
Fellow Worker, is now plush.
As the dark deepens I walk
Out Wentworth, grit under my feet.
The smell of frying potatoes
Seeps through the dirty windows.
The old red light district is
Mostly torn down, vacant lots
Line the railroad tracks. I know
What Marvell meant by desarts
Of vast eternitie. Man
Gets daily sicker and his
Ugliness knots his bowels.
On the sight of several
Splendid historical brothels
Stands the production plant of
Time-Luce Incorporated.
Die Ausrottung der Besten.

Do not cut a hole in the
Side of a boat to mark the
Place where your sword dropped and sank.

. . . .

II

. . . .

Discursive knowledge, knowledge by
Indirection passes away
And love, knowledge by direction,
Directly of another, grows
In its place. There exists a point
At which the known passes through
A sort of occultation,
A zero between plus and
Minus in which knower and known
And their knowledge cease to exist.
Perfect love casts out knowledge.

The Pont du Gard as beautiful
As ever. Why can't a culture
Of businessmen and engineers
Make beautiful things? I walk
Across on top and then back
Under the small arches with
Idyllic frames of Provence
Slipping past me and suddenly
I notice the shells in the rock—
With my head full of the
Fossils of a million years,
Standing on this fossilized
Roman engineering, built of
Mudflats of fossil seas, springing
From cliffs with caves of fossil man—
Half-naked jeunesse with golden
Bodies scamper over golden
Stone, the air is full of swallows
Whirling above flowing water.

There are three ways of loving,
Modes of communication,
The realization via
The ground of possibility,

We touch each other through the
Material of love, the earth
Center which all share; or by means
Of ultimate inclusive
Action, the empyrean
Shared by all persons where the
Mythology and drama
Of the person is realized
In pure archetype; or face
To face in the act of love,
Which for most men is the way
In which the other modes are
Raised into consciousness and
Into a measure of control.

Provence hot, the hills grey with heat,
Miles of olive trees, silver green,
The color of Sung celadon,
The houses peach colored, over
Each doorway a grape vine, around
It the wall stained pale blue-green with
Copper sulphate spray. Avignon,
Beautiful across the river
But with a god damned visite;
(The legends and chauvinism
Of an ancien combattant,
Permitted, because he has given
A leg or arm to France to beg
In this tedious way. Splendid
Fellows, salty and wise, as who
Wouldn't have to be if this
Was all he got from a grateful
People, but hardly the screen
Through which to absorb The Past.)
And over all the lingering
Stink of the Papacy and
The present stink of English tourists.

The vélos roll down hill, mile
After mile beside rushing
Water into Aix. We go for
A swim in the cold piscine at
The Roman baths and on into
That city of small splendors.

Seldom has man made so perfect
A work of art of light and shade.
The Fromentins are fine in the
Cathedral, but they can't compare
With the green submarine light
Of the Cours Mirabeau broken
By pools of clarity at the
Small fountains at the crossings,
The dark gloom and black statue
Of King René at one end,
The white glare of the Fountain
Of Culture at the other.
Certainly the most civilized
Man ever to get mixed up
With a revolution has
An elegant monument.

The author of *Le Rideau levé*,
Approached as a colleague by
Sade in prison, repulsed him
Succinctly, "Mon Sieur, je ne suis
Pas ici pour avoir donné des
Confits empoisonnés aux femmes
De chambre." The existentialistes
Don't like him very much.

Granet painting in Rome, never
Forgot that light and shade. In
The museum his paintings with
Their stereoscopic values
Hang by his two portraits—
The famous Ingres, more handsome
Than Byron, and another
Of an old, old, dying man.

Lots of Cézanne watercolors
Full of peach blossoms and leaf flicker.

Milhaud, Cendrars, Tal-Coat, a place
Where men with balls can escape
The maggots of the Deux Magots.

Dinner at the Café Mistral,
Plover's eggs and tomatillos
In aspic, écrevisse, raw tuna
With chives, thick noodles with saffron,
Duckling with truffles and cèpes,
Fricassée of guinea hen,
A local wine, not still, not
Sparkling, but volatile like
The chiantis of Florence,
A dark blue cheese, and black, black
Coffee and Rémy Martin
And thick layers of cream—
And then like all the world we
Promenade on Mirabeau's
Fine street and eat glaces and
Drink more cognac and coffee.
At last the strange malady
Of France has vanished and the
Women once more are mammals.

At last the ability to
Know directly becomes a
Habit of the soul and the
Dominant mode in which
Possibility is presented
To the developing person.
As such it ceases to appear
As consequence and becomes
Conscious communion with a
Person. A duality
Is established which focuses
The reflection of the mountain
As an illuminating ray

On the mountain itself,
The moon dissolves in the water
Held in the palm of the hand.

. . . .

III

. . . .

Boswell: "Sir, what is the chief
Virtue?" Johnson: "Courage, Sir,
Without it, opportunity
To exercise the others
Will often be found wanting."

On his first visit to the States,
Wells was asked what most impressed him.
He said, "The female schoolteachers.
In two generations they will
Destroy the country." It took one.

In the Uffizi I prefer
To spend most of my time with the
Even tempered Greeks and Romans.
Pictures in galleries always
Look to me like dressed meat in
Butcher shops. From Cimabue
And Simone Martini,
Arrows point across the river
To Bronzino, and via
Raphael, to Picasso.
Without Florence, there isn't
Really any modern painting,
But just the same, it looks cooked.
Straight through, from beginning to end,
It is all Mannerism.

In the churches you get tired
Of all the Taddis and Gaddis.
Why does no one ever point out
That the great Masaccios are
Compounded of the elements
Of Roman painting, and no
Others at all, and that each figure
Is derived from classic sculpture?
There is the same knowledge of
Good and evil, and in the face
Of it, the same serenity.

God is that person who
Satisfies all love, with whom
Indwelling encompasses
All reality. It is
Impossible to say if there
Exists only one god, the
Ultimate beloved of all
Persons. It would seem rather,
Since the relationship is
Reciprocal and progressive,
That there are as many gods
As lovers. Theoretically
One infinite god could
Satisfy all finite lovers—
But this concept comes from the
Insoluble residues of
The quantitative mathematics
Of infinitudes. It really
Has no place in the discussion
Of the love relationship,
Which knows neither finite nor
Infinite. The Shekinah
And Jehovah are only
An enlarged mirror image
Of the terrestrial embrace.
The sephiroth of the Kabbalah
Are the chakras of the Tantra.
The records of Hafidh, Rumi,

St. Theresa, even the crazed
Augustine, seem to be the
Records in each case of a
Unique duality. The
Object of love is a person
Like the lover, and the demands
On the definition of
A monotheistic god
Made by other philosophical
Considerations, largely
Of an arithmetical
Nature, make it unlikely
That such an entity could be
Also a person. There is here a
Collision of two exclusive
Modes of viewing reality.
Hence perhaps the peculiar
Subjective tension of the
Monotheistic mystic,
The reason why he always feels
His love as incomplete and
Destructive of his person.

Agathias Scholasticus:
Restless and discontent
I lie awake all night long.
And as I drowse in the dawn,
The swallows stir in the eaves,
And wake me weeping again.
I press my eyes close tight, but
Your face rises before me.
O birds, be quiet with
Your tittering accusations.
I did not cut that dead girl's tongue.
Go weep for her lover in the hills,
Cry by the hoopoe's nest in the rocks.
Let me sleep for a while, and dream
I lie once more in my girl's arms.

Under a lattice of leaves
Her white thighs in cloth of gold
That casts a glittering shade.
She turned to her left and stared at
The sun. My imagination
Was moved by her gesture, and as
I turned, I saw the sun
Sparkle all round, like iron
Pulled molten from the furnace.

Bright petals of evening
Shatter, fall, drift over Florence,
And flush your cheeks a redder
Rose and gleam like fiery flakes
In your eyes. All over Florence
The swallows whirl between the
Tall roofs, under the bridge arches,
Spiral in the zenith like larks,
Sweep low in crying clouds above
The brown river and the white
River bed. Your moist, quivering
Lips are like the wet scarlet wings
Of a reborn butterfly who
Trembles on the rose petal as
Life floods his strange body.
Turn to me. Part your lips. My dear,
Some day we will be dead.

I feel like Pascal often felt.

About the mid houre of the nicht ꞌ

FIRE

The air is dizzy with swallows.

Sunset comes on the golden
Towers, on the Signoría.
In the Badía, the light goes
From the face of Filippino's

Weary lady, exhausted with
The devotion of her worshipper.
Across the face of the Duomo
The Campanile's blue shadow
Marks the mathematics of beauty.
In San Miniato the gold
Mosaics still glitter through
The smoky gloom. At the end
Of the Way of the Cross, the dense
Cypress wood, full of lovers,
Shivering with impatience.
As the dark thickens, two by two
They take each other. Nightfall, all
The wood is filled with soft moaning,
As though it were filled with doves.

. . . .

Michelangelo was surely
A noisy man, and terribly
Conceited. After all, nothing
Ever happened to him that
Doesn't happen to all of us.
If you have tragedy to
Portray, you should be humble
About it, you are serving
The bread of communion.
"Too many nakeds for a chapel,"
Said Evelyn. But I don't think it
Was the exposed privates of the
Mother of God made the Pope faint.
That's an arrogant, perverse, pride
Soaked wall, a good thing to look down
On the election of the Popes.
Maybe he intended it for
A portrait of the Papacy.
But the Moses was beautiful
Just before the church shut, looking
Like oiled ivory against
The wavering blackness in
The light of the vigil lamps.

The worship of art, the attempt
To substitute it for religion,
Is the blindest superstition
Of them all. Almost all works of
Art are failures. The successes
Occur hardly once in a
Lifetime even in periods
Of great cultural flowering;
And then they are likely to be
Unpretentious perfections,
Of modest scope, exquisite
As a delicate wine and
Often no more significant.
Better lump them all together—
"A good judge of wine, women,
And horseflesh"—than go posting
For the Absolute in the
Galleries of Fifty-seventh Street—
Or the Louvre—or the Uffizi.
The World's Masterpieces are
Too often by Vasari,
Benjamin West, Picasso,
Or Diego Rivera.

The Pope was once content to rule
The rulers, the masses were
Allowed their old worship under
A new nomenclature. Feudal
Methods of exploitation
Required a homogeneous
Society, a "natural"
Religion. New methods,
New cadres. Capitalism
Revived all the paranoid
Compulsions of rabbinical
Judaism, coupled with
A schizophrenic doctrine
Of the person as utterly
Alone, subsistent as a pure
Integer at the will of a

Uniquely self subsistent
Commander (hardly a lover),
Two things with wills. It required
The total atomization
Of society. The family
Hierarchy disappeared and the
Monogamous couple was
Substituted. Not a vehicle
Of mystic love, but an iron
Necessity for survival.

Says Evelyn, "Turning to the right
Out of the Porta del Popolo,
We came to Justinian's
Gardens, near the Muro Torto,
So prominently built as to
Threaten to fall any moment,
Yet standing so these thousand years.
Under this is the burying
Place of the common prostitutes,
Where they are put into the ground
Sans ceremony." In the
Rotonda Sant' Agostino,
A sign, "Whores will refrain
From hustling the customers
During their devotions." From the
Albergo Inghilterra
To the Piazza di Spagna
Stretches a solid tide wall
Of crew-cut American fairies,
Elderly nymphomaniacs,
Double breasted, gabardined
Artisti. The latter have reduced
Hemingway to a formula.
"Let's go," Bill said. "Let's go," Pete said.
"OK, let's go," Joe said. It's like
Dante's terza rima, and the
Triad of the dialectic.
Honest. They write books about it.
Everybody on the prowl

For Cineasti and Milioni
Of any sex. The Via
Vittorio Veneto
After dark is strictly graded.
On the terrace of the Doni
Sit the condottieri of
The Marshall Plan like Rameses.
The Cineasti and Milioni
Lounge over their highballs.
The artisti stand and bow.
The more expensive whores walk
The sidewalks. The poorer whores work
The side streets. The most expensive
Sit. At the entrance to the
Park are whores from Masereel
And Félicien Rops. Inside are
Italian boys who get paid.
Further inside are beringed
Cigar smoking Italians, who
All look like Mussolini's
Grandfather. They will pay you.
At the beginning of the street
Is the American Embassy.
Midway is an ESSO pump.
At the end is the devouring dark.

"La mauvaise conscience des
Bourgeois, ai-je dit, a paralysé
Tout le mouvement intellectuel
Et moral de la bourgeoisie.
Je me corrige, et je remplace
Ce mot 'paralysé' par
Cet autre: 'dénaturé.' "
So Bakunin says, and Marx,
"The bourgeoisie, wherever
It has got the upper hand,
Has put an end to all feudal,
Patriarchal, idyllic
Relations. It has pitilessly
Torn asunder the motley

Feudal ties that bound man to
His 'natural superiors,'
And has left no other nexus
Between man and man than naked
Self interest, than callous
Cash payment. It has drowned the
Most heavenly ecstasies
Of religious fervor, of
Chivalrous enthusiasm,
Of philistine sentimentalism,
In the icy water of
Egotistical calculation.
It has resolved personal worth
Into exchange value, and in
Place of the numberless
Indefeasible chartered freedoms,
Has set up that single
Unconscionable freedom,
Free trade. In a word, for
Exploitation veiled by
Religious and political
Illusions, it has substituted
Naked, shameless, direct, brutal
Exploitation."
For Dante,
Usury was the ultimate
Form of pederasty, in which
Buggery attempts to make
Its turds its heirs.

Sexual fulfillment was robbed
Of all meaning. The sex act became
A nervous stimulant and
Anodyne outside of the
Productive process, but still
Necessary to it as an
Insatiable, irrational
Drive, without which the struggle
For meaningless abstractions,
Commodities, would collapse.

This is the ultimate in
Human self alienation.
This is what the revolution
Is about. In a society
Ruled only by the cash nexus
The sexual relationship
Must be a continual struggle
Of each to obtain security
From the other, a kind of
Security, a mass of
Commodities, which has no
Meaning for love, and today in
America, no meaning at all.
The greater the mass of things,
The greater the insecurity.
The security of love lies
In the state of indwelling rest.
It is its own security.
This is what free love is, freedom
From the destructive power
Of a society coerced
Into the pursuit of insane
Objectives. Until men learn
To administer things, and are
No longer themselves organized
And exploited as things, there can
Be no love except by intense
Effort directed against
The whole pressure of the world.
In other words, love becomes,
As it was with the Gnostics,
The practice of a kind of cult.
Against it are arrayed all
The consequences of a
Vast systematic delusion,
Without intelligence or
Mercy or even real being,
But with the power to kill.

. . . .

America is today a
Nation profoundly deranged,
Demented, and sick, because
Americans with very few
Exceptions believe, or when
They doubt are terrified to
Be discovered doubting, that
Love is measured entirely
In an interchange of
Commodities. The wife provides
Pop-up toast, synthetic coffee,
Frozen orange juice, two eggs of
Standard color, size, and flavor,
In the morning, at night the
Fantastic highly-colored canned
Poisons which grace the cooking
And advertising pages
Of the women's magazines.
In exchange the husband provides
Her with the clothes and cosmetics
Of a movie courtesan,
A vast array of "labor"
Saving devices, all streamlined,
Presumably so they can be
Thrown, a car, never more than
Two years old, engineered with
Great skill to their social status,
A television set, a dream
House, designed by a fairy,
And built of glass and cardboard,
A bathroom full of cramped, pastel
Tinted plumbing. When they wish
To satisfy their passions,
They go to a movie. The
Sexual relation is
A momentary lapse from
The routine fulfillment of
This vision, which is portrayed
As love and marriage by thousands
Of decorticated and

Debauched intellectuals,
Who enjoy the incomes of princes.
Almost all advertising
In America today
Is aimed at the young married
Couple. Billions are consciously
And deliberately spent
To destroy love at its source.
Like the "fiends" who are picked up
In parks, an advertising
Man is a professional
Murderer of young lovers—
On an infinitely vaster scale.

You will find more peace and more
Communion, more love, in an hour
In the arms of a pickup in
Singapore or Reykjavik,
Than you will find in a lifetime
Married to a middle class
White American woman.

It feels like it's made of plastic.
It smells like it's perfumed with
Coal tar. It tastes like it's made
Of soybeans. It looks like an
Abandoned pee-wee golf course.
It is still and sterile
As a crater on the moon.

Sitting there, reading this in your
Psychoanalyst's waiting room,
Thirty-five years old, faintly
Perfumed, expensively dressed,
Sheer nylons strapped to freezing thighs,
Brain removed at Bennington
Or Sarah Lawrence, dutiful
Reader of the *Partisan*
Review's Book of the Month, target
Of my highbrow publisher, you

Think this is all just Art—contrast—
Naples—New York. It is not. Every time
You open your frigidaire
A dead Neapolitan baby
Drops out. Your world is not crazy.
But dead. It can only mimic
Life with the economics of
Murder. "War production and
Colonialization of
The former imperialist
Centers." This is the definition
Of Fascism. You are not just
Responsible. You are the dead
Neapolitan baby,
The other side of the coin.
I don't wonder you've never
Been the same since you left the
Tickets to *Don Giovanni*
In the orgone collector.

. . . .

Paestum, the apex of the trip,
And the zenith of our years.

Helen's jewel, the Schethya,
The Taoist uncut block,
The stone of the alchemist,
The footstool of Elohim's throne,
Which they hurled into the Abyss,
On which stands the queen and sacred
Whore, Malkuth, the stone which served
Jacob for pillow and altar.

"And what is truth?" said Pilate,
"A,E,I,O,U—the spheres
Of the planets, the heavens'
Pentachord. A noir, E blanc,
I rouge, O bleu, U vert."

When in Japan, the goddess
Of the sun, attracted by
The obscene gestures of the flesh,
Came out from eclipse, she spoke
The first and oldest mystery,
"1, 2, 3, 4, 5, 6, 7,
8, 9, 10."

All things have a name.
Every mote in the sunlight has
A name, and the sunlight itself
Has a name, and the spirit who
Troubles the waters has a name.

As the Philosopher says,
"The Pythagoreans are
Of the opinion that the shapes
Of the Greek vase are reflections
Of the irrational numbers
Thought by the Pure Mind. On the
Other hand, the Epicureans
Hold them to be derived
From the curves of a girl's
Breasts and thighs and buttocks."

The doctrine of Signatures—
The law by which we must make
Use of things is written in
The law by which they were made.
It is graven upon each
As its unique character.
The forms of being are the
Rules of life.

The Smaragdine Tablet
Says, "That which is above is
Reflected in that which is below."

Paestum of the twice blooming
Roses, the sea god's honey-

Colored stone still strong against
The folly of the long decline
Of man. The snail climbs the Doric
Line, and the empty snail shell
Lies by the wild cyclamen.
The sandstone of the Roman
Road is marked with sun wrinkles
Of prehistoric beaches,
But no time at all has touched
The deep constant melodies
Of space as the columns swing
To the moving eye. The sea
Breathes like a drowsy woman.
The sun moves like a drowsy hand.
Poseidon's pillars have endured
All tempers of the sea and sun.
This is the order of the spheres,
The curve of the unwinding fern,
And the purple shell in the sea;
These are the spaces of the notes
Of every kind of music.
The world is made of number
And moved in order by love.
Mankind has risen to this point
And can only fall away,
As we can only turn homeward
Up Italy, through France, to life
Always pivoted on this place.

Sweet Anyte of Tegea—
"The children have put purple
Reins on you, he goat, and a
Bridle in your bearded mouth.
And they play at horse races
Round a temple where a god
Gazes on their childish joy."

Finally the few tourists go,
The German photographers, the
Bevy of seminarians,

And we are left alone. We eat
In the pronaos towards the sea.
Greek food, small white loaves, smoked cheese,
Pickled squid, black figs, and honey
And olive oil, the common food
Of Naples, still, for those who eat.
An ancient dog, Odysseus' dog,
Spawned before there were breeds of dogs,
Appears, begs, eats, and disappears—
The exoteric proxy of
The god. And we too grow drowsy with
White wine, tarry from the wineskin.
The blue and gold shafts interweave
Across our nodding eyes. The sea
Prepares to take the sun. We go
Into the naos, open to the
Sky and make love, where the sea god
And the sea goddess, wet with sperm,
Coupled in the incense filled dark,
As the singing rose and was still.

Mist comes with the sunset. (The Yanks
Killed the mosquitoes.) Long lines of
Umber buffalo, their backs a
Rippling congruence, as in the
Paintings of Krishna, file across
The brilliant green sea meadows,
Under banners of white mist.
The fires of the bivouacs of
Spartacus twinkle in the hills.
Our train comes with the first stars.
Venus over the wine dark sea.

All the way back the train fills
And fills up, and fills again,
With girls from the fish canneries,
And girls from the lace factories,
And girls from the fields, who have been
Working twelve hours for nothing,
Or at the best a few pennies.

ʒh and sing, all the way
ʳaples, like broad bottomed,
med angels, wet with sweat.

⌄cret place
⌐ɾay human love perfect itself.

. . . .

V

I come back to the cottage in
Santa Monica Canyon where
Andrée and I were poor and
Happy together. Sometimes we
Were hungry and stole vegetables
From the neighbors' gardens.
Sometimes we went out and gathered
Cigarette butts by flashlight.
But we went swimming every day,
All year round. We had a dog
Called Proclus, a vast yellow
Mongrel, and a white cat named
Cyprian. We had our first
Joint art show, and they began
To publish my poems in Paris.
We worked under the low umbrella
Of the acacia in the dooryard.
Now I get out of the car
And stand before the house in the dusk.
The acacia blossoms powder the walk
With little pills of gold wool.
The odor is drowsy and thick
In the early evening.
The tree has grown twice as high
As the roof. Inside, an old man
And woman sit in the lamplight.
I go back and drive away
To Malibu Beach and sit
With a grey-haired childhood friend and

Watch the full moon rise over the
Long rollers wrinkling the dark bay.

"It is those who are married
Who should live the contemplative
Life together. In the world
There is the long day of
Destruction to go by. But
Let those who are single, man
Torn from woman, woman from
Man, men altogether, women
Altogether, separate
Deathly fragments, each returning
And adhering to its own kind,
The body of life torn in two,
Let these finish the day of
Destruction, and those who have
United go into the
Wilderness to know a new
Heaven and a new earth."

There are those who spend all their lives
Whirling in the love and hate
Of the deities they create.

Contemplation is direct
Knowledge, beyond consequence,
Ignorance, appetite, grasping
Of possibility. The
Contemplative knows himself
As the focus of the others,
And he knows the other, the
Dual, as the mirror of
Himself and all the others,
The others as the mirror
Of himself and the dual.

. . . .

As long as we are lost
In the world of purpose
We are not free. I sit
In my ten foot square hut.
The birds sing. The bees hum.
The leaves sway. The water
Murmurs over the rocks.
The canyon shuts me in.
If I moved, Bashō's frog
Would splash in the pool.
All Summer long the gold
Laurel leaves fell through space.
Today I was aware
Of a maple leaf floating
On the pool. In the night
I stare into the fire.
Once I saw fire cities,
Towns, palaces, wars,
Heroic adventures,
In the campfires of youth.
Now I see only fire.
My breath moves quietly.
The stars move overhead.
In the clear darkness
Only a small red glow
Is left in the ashes.
On the table lies a cast
Snakeskin and an uncut stone.

There is no need to assume
The existence of a god
Behind the community
Of persons, the community
Is the absolute. There is no
Future life because there is
No future. Reality
Is not conditioned by time,
Space, ignorance, grasping.
The shift from possibility
To consequence gives rise to

The convention of time. At
The heart of being is the act of
Contemplation, it is timeless.

Since Isis and Osiris
Many gods and goddesses
Have ridden the boats of
The sun and the moon. I stand
On the hill above my hut
And watch the sun set in the
Fog bank over the distant
Ocean. Shortly afterward
The moon rises, transparent
In the twilight above the
Mountain. There is nobody
In them this evening. I
Am sure they are empty, that
I am alone in the great
Void, where they journey, empty
Through the darkness and the light.

Deep in myself arise the rays
Called Artemis and Apollo,
Helios, Luna, Sun and Moon,
Flowing forever out into
The void, towards the unknown others.

The heavens and hells of man,
The gods and demons, the ghosts of
Superstition, are crude attempts;
The systems of philosophers,
The visions of religion,
Are more or less successful
Mythological descriptions
Of knowing, acting, loving—
You are Shiva, but you dream.

It is the dark of the moon.
Late at night, the end of Summer,
The Autumn constellations

Glow in the arid heaven.
The air smells of cattle, hay,
And dust. In the old orchard
The pears are ripe. The trees
Have sprouted from old rootstocks
And the fruit is inedible.
As I pass them I hear something
Rustling and grunting and turn
My light into the branches.
Two raccoons with acrid pear
Juice and saliva drooling
From their mouths, stare back at me,
Their eyes deep sponges of light.
They know me and do not run
Away. Coming up the road
Through the black oak shadows, I
See ahead of me, glinting
Everywhere from the dusty
Gravel, tiny points of cold
Blue light, like the sparkle of
Iron snow. I suspect what it is,
And kneel to see. Under each
Pebble and oak leaf is a
Spider, her eyes shining at
Me with my reflected light
Across immeasurable distance.

from SEVEN POEMS FOR MARTHE, MY WIFE

THE REFLECTING TREES
OF BEING AND NOT BEING

In my childhood when I first
Saw myself unfolded in
The triple mirrors, in my
Youth, when I pursued myself
Wandering on wandering
Nightbound roads like a roving
Masterless dog, when I met
Myself on sharp peaks of ice,
And tasted myself dissolved
In the lulling heavy sea,
In the talking night, in the
Spiraling stars, what did I
Know? What do I know now,
Of myself, of the others?
Blood flows out to the fleeing
Nebulae, and flows back, red
With all the worn space of space,
Old with all the time of time.
It is my blood. I cannot
Taste in it as it leaves me
More of myself than on its
Return. I can see in it
Trees of silence and fire.
In the mirrors on its waves
I can see faces. Mostly
They are your face. On its streams
I can see the soft moonlight
On the Canal du Midi.
I can see the leaf shadows
Of the plane trees on the deep
Fluids of your eyes, and the
Golden fires and lamps of years.

MARTHE AWAY (SHE IS AWAY)

All night I lay awake beside you,
Leaning on my elbow, watching your
Sleeping face, that face whose purity
Never ceases to astonish me.
I could not sleep. But I did not want
Sleep nor miss it. Against my body,
Your body lay like a warm soft star.
How many nights I have waked and watched
You, in how many places. Who knows?
This night might be the last one of all.
As on so many nights, once more I
Drank from your sleeping flesh the deep still
Communion I am not always strong
Enough to take from you waking, the peace of love.
Foggy lights moved over the ceiling
Of our room, so like the rooms of France
And Italy, rooms of honeymoon,
And gave your face an ever changing
Speech, the secret communication
Of untellable love. I knew then,
As your secret spoke, my secret self,
The blind bird, hardly visible in
An endless web of lies. And I knew
The web too, its every knot and strand,
The hidden crippled bird, the terrible web.
Towards the end of night, as trucks rumbled
In the streets, you stirred, cuddled to me,
And spoke my name. Your voice was the voice
Of a girl who had never known loss
Of love, betrayal, mistrust, or lie.
And later you turned again and clutched
My hand and pressed it to your body.
Now I know surely and forever,
However much I have blotted our
Waking love, its memory is still
There. And I know the web, the net,
The blind and crippled bird. For then, for
One brief instant it was not blind, nor

Trapped, nor crippled. For one heart beat the
Heart was free and moved itself. O love,
I who am lost and damned with words,
Whose words are a business and an art,
I have no words. These words, this poem, this
Is all confusion and ignorance.
But I know that coached by your sweet heart,
My heart beat one free beat and sent
Through all my flesh the blood of truth.

A DIALOGUE OF WATCHING

Let me celebrate you. I
Have never known anyone
More beautiful than you. I
Walking beside you, watching
You move beside me, watching
That still grace of hand and thigh,
Watching your face change with words
You do not say, watching your
Solemn eyes as they turn to me,
Or turn inward, full of knowing,
Slow or quick, watching your full
Lips part and smile or turn grave,
Watching your narrow waist, your
Proud buttocks in their grace, like
A sailing swan, an animal,
Free, your own, and never
To be subjugated, but
Abandoned, as I am to you,
Overhearing your perfect
Speech of motion, of love and
Trust and security as
You feed or play with our children.
I have never known any
One more beautiful than you.

from THE LIGHTS IN THE SKY ARE STARS

for Mary

HALLEY'S COMET

When in your middle years
The great comet comes again
Remember me, a child,
Awake in the summer night,
Standing in my crib and
Watching that long-haired star
So many years ago.
Go out in the dark and see
Its plume over water
Dribbling on the liquid night,
And think that life and glory
Flickered on the rushing
Bloodstream for me once, and for
All who have gone before me,
Vessels of the billion-year-long
River that flows now in your veins.

THE GREAT NEBULA
OF ANDROMEDA

We get into camp after
Dark, high on an open ridge
Looking out over five thousand
Feet of mountains and mile
Beyond mile of valley and sea.
In the star-filled dark we cook
Our macaroni and eat
By lantern light. Stars cluster
Around our table like fireflies.
After supper we go straight
To bed. The night is windy
And clear. The moon is three days
Short of full. We lie in bed
And watch the stars and the turning

Moon through our little telescope.
Late at night the horses stumble
Around camp and I awake.
I lie on my elbow watching
Your beautiful sleeping face
Like a jewel in the moonlight.
If you are lucky and the
Nations let you, you will live
Far into the twenty-first
Century. I pick up the glass
And watch the Great Nebula
Of Andromeda swim like
A phosphorescent amoeba
Slowly around the Pole. Far
Away in distant cities
Fat-hearted men are planning
To murder you while you sleep.

A SWORD IN A CLOUD
OF LIGHT

Your hand in mine, we walk out
To watch the Christmas Eve crowds
On Fillmore Street, the Negro
District. The night is thick with
Frost. The people hurry, wreathed
In their smoky breaths. Before
The shop windows the children
Jump up and down with spangled
Eyes. Santa Clauses ring bells.
Cars stall and honk. Street cars clang.
Loud speakers on the lampposts
Sing carols, on juke boxes
In the bars Louis Armstrong
Plays *White Christmas*. In the joints
The girls strip and grind and bump
To *Jingle Bells*. Overhead
The neon signs scribble and
Erase and scribble again

Messages of avarice,
Joy, fear, hygiene, and the proud
Names of the middle classes.
The moon beams like a pudding.
We stop at the main corner
And look up, diagonally
Across, at the rising moon,
And the solemn, orderly
Vast winter constellations.
You say, "There's Orion!"
The most beautiful object
Either of us will ever
Know in the world or in life
Stands in the moonlit empty
Heavens, over the swarming
Men, women, and children, black
And white, joyous and greedy,
Evil and good, buyer and
Seller, master and victim,
Like some immense theorem,
Which, if once solved would forever
Solve the mystery and pain
Under the bells and spangles.
There he is, the man of the
Night before Christmas, spread out
On the sky like a true god
In whom it would only be
Necessary to believe
A little. I am fifty
And you are five. It would do
No good to say this and it
May do no good to write it.
Believe in Orion. Believe
In the night, the moon, the crowded
Earth. Believe in Christmas and
Birthdays and Easter rabbits.
Believe in all those fugitive
Compounds of nature, all doomed
To waste away and go out.
Always be true to these things.
They are all there is. Never

Give up this savage religion
For the blood-drenched civilized
Abstractions of the rascals
Who live by killing you and me.

A LIVING PEARL

At sixteen I came West, riding
Freights on the Chicago, Milwaukee
And St. Paul, the Great Northern,
The Northern Pacific. I got
A job as helper to a man
Who gathered wild horses in the
Mass drives in the Okanogan
And Horse Heaven country. The best
We culled out as part profit from
The drive, the rest went for chicken
And dog feed. We took thirty head
Up the Methow, up the Twisp,
Across the headwaters of Lake
Chelan, down the Skagit to
The Puget Sound country. I
Did the cooking and camp work.
In a couple of weeks I
Could handle the stock pretty well.
Every day we saddled and rode
A new horse. Next day we put a
Packsaddle on him. By the
Time we reached Marblemount
We considered them well broken.
The scissorbills who bought them
Considered them untamed mustangs
Of the desert. In a few weeks
They were peacefully pulling
Milk wagons in Sedro-Wooley.
We made three trips a season

And did well enough for the
Post-war depression.
Tonight,
Thirty years later, I walk
Out of the deserted miner's
Cabin in Mono Pass, under
The full moon and the few large stars.
The sidehills are piebald with snow.
The midnight air is suffused
With moonlight. As Dante says,
"It is as though a cloud enclosed
Me, lucid, dense, solid, polished,
Like a diamond forged by the sun.
We entered the eternal pearl,
Which took us as water takes
A ray of light, itself uncleft."
Fifteen years ago, in this place,
I wrote a poem called "Toward
An Organic Philosophy."
Everything is still the same,
And it differs very little
From the first mountain pass I
Crossed so long ago with the
Pintos and zebra duns and
Gunmetal roans and buckskins,
And splattered lallapaloosas,
The stocky wild ponies whose
Ancestors came with Coronado.
There are no horse bells tonight,
Only the singing of frogs
In the snow-wet meadows, the shrill
Single bark of a mountain
Fox, high in the rocks where the
Wild sheep move silently through the
Crystal moonlight. The same feelings
Come back. Once more all the awe
Of a boy from the prairies where
Lanterns move through the comfortable
Dark, along a fence, through a field,
Home; all the thrill of youth

Suddenly come from the flat
Geometrical streets of
Chicago, into the illimitable
And inhuman waste places
Of the Far West, where the mind finds
Again the forms Pythagoras
Sought, the organic relations
Of stone and cloud and flower
And moving planet and falling
Water. Marthe and Mary sleep
In their down bags, cocoons of
Mutual love. Half my life has
Been passed in the West, much of it
On the ground beside lonely fires
Under the summer stars, and in
Cabins where the snow drifted through
The pines and over the roof.
I will not camp here as often
As I have before. Thirty years
Will never come for me again.
"Our campfire dies out in the
Lonely mountains. The transparent
Moonlight stretches a thousand miles.
The clear peace is without end."
My daughter's deep blue eyes sleep
In the moon shadow. Next week
She will be one year old.

FOR ELI JACOBSON

December, 1952

There are few of us now, soon
There will be none. We were comrades
Together, we believed we
Would see with our own eyes the new
World where man was no longer
Wolf to man, but men and women

Were all brothers and lovers
Together. We will not see it.
We will not see it, none of us.
It is farther off than we thought.
In our young days we believed
That as we grew old and fell
Out of rank, new recruits, young
And with the wisdom of youth,
Would take our places and they
Surely would grow old in the
Golden Age. They have not come.
They will not come. There are not
Many of us left. Once we
Marched in closed ranks, today each
Of us fights off the enemy,
A lonely isolated guerrilla.
All this has happened before,
Many times. It does not matter.
We were comrades together.
Life was good for us. It is
Good to be brave — nothing is
Better. Food tastes better. Wine
Is more brilliant. Girls are more
Beautiful. The sky is bluer
For the brave — for the brave and
Happy comrades and for the
Lonely brave retreating warriors.
You had a good life. Even all
Its sorrows and defeats and
Disillusionments were good,
Met with courage and a gay heart.
You are gone and we are that
Much more alone. We are one fewer,
Soon we shall be none. We know now
We have failed for a long time.
And we do not care. We few will
Remember as long as we can,
Our children may remember,
Some day the world will remember.
Then they will say, "They lived in

The days of the good comrades.
It must have been wonderful
To have been alive then, though it
Is very beautiful now."
We will be remembered, all
Of us, always, by all men,
In the good days now so far away.
If the good days never come,
We will not know. We will not care.
Our lives were the best. We were the
Happiest men alive in our day.

THE BAD OLD DAYS

The summer of nineteen eighteen
I read *The Jungle* and *The
Research Magnificent*. That fall
My father died and my aunt
Took me to Chicago to live.
The first thing I did was to take
A streetcar to the stockyards.
In the winter afternoon,
Gritty and fetid, I walked
Through the filthy snow, through the
Squalid streets, looking shyly
Into the people's faces,
Those who were home in the daytime.
Debauched and exhausted faces,
Starved and looted brains, faces
Like the faces in the senile
And insane wards of charity
Hospitals. Predatory
Faces of little children.
Then as the soiled twilight darkened,
Under the green gas lamps, and the
Sputtering purple arc lamps,
The faces of the men coming

Home from work, some still alive with
The last pulse of hope or courage,
Some sly and bitter, some smart and
Silly, most of them already
Broken and empty, no life,
Only blinding tiredness, worse
Than any tired animal.
The sour smells of a thousand
Suppers of fried potatoes and
Fried cabbage bled into the street.
I was giddy and sick, and out
Of my misery I felt rising
A terrible anger and out
Of the anger, an absolute vow.
Today the evil is clean
And prosperous, but it is
Everywhere, you don't have to
Take a streetcar to find it,
And it is the same evil.
And the misery, and the
Anger, and the vow are the same.

from MARY AND THE SEASONS

SPRING RAIN

The smoke of our campfire lowers
And coagulates under
The redwoods, like low-lying
Clouds. Fine mist fills the air. Drops
Rattle down from all the leaves.
As the evening comes on
The treetops vanish in fog.
Two saw-whet owls utter their
Metallic sobbing cries high
Overhead. As it gets dark
The mist turns to rain. We are

All alone in the forest.
No one is near us for miles.
In the firelight mice scurry
Hunting crumbs. Tree toads cry like
Tiny owls. Deer snort in the
Underbrush. Their eyes are green
In the firelight like balls of
Foxfire. This morning I read
Mei Yao Chen's poems, all afternoon
We walked along the stream through
Woods and meadows full of June
Flowers. We chased frogs in the
Pools and played with newts and young
Grass snakes. I picked a wild rose
For your hair. You brought
New flowers for me to name.
Now it is night and our fire
Is a red throat open in
The profound blackness, full of
The throb and hiss of the rain.

THOU SHALT NOT KILL

A Memorial for Dylan Thomas

I

They are murdering all the young men.
For half a century now, every day,
They have hunted them down and killed them.
They are killing them now.
At this minute, all over the world,
They are killing the young men.
They know ten thousand ways to kill them.
Every year they invent new ones.
In the jungles of Africa,
In the marshes of Asia,
In the deserts of Asia,
In the slave pens of Siberia,
In the slums of Europe,
In the nightclubs of America,
The murderers are at work.

They are stoning Stephen,
They are casting him forth from every city in the world.
Under the Welcome sign,
Under the Rotary emblem,
On the highway in the suburbs,
His body lies under the hurling stones.
He was full of faith and power.
He did great wonders among the people.
They could not stand against his wisdom.
They could not bear the spirit with which he spoke.
He cried out in the name
Of the tabernacle of witness in the wilderness.
They were cut to the heart.
They gnashed against him with their teeth.
They cried out with a loud voice.
They stopped their ears.

They ran on him with one accord.
They cast him out of the city and stoned him.
The witnesses laid down their clothes
At the feet of a man whose name was your name —
You.

You are the murderer.
You are killing the young men.
You are broiling Lawrence on his gridiron.
When you demanded he divulge
The hidden treasures of the spirit,
He showed you the poor.
You set your heart against him.
You seized him and bound him with rage.
You roasted him on a slow fire.
His fat dripped and spurted in the flame.
The smell was sweet to your nose.
He cried out,
"I am cooked on this side,
Turn me over and eat,
You
Eat of my flesh."

You are murdering the young men.
You are shooting Sebastian with arrows.
He kept the faithful steadfast under persecution.
First you shot him with arrows.
Then you beat him with rods.
Then you threw him in a sewer.
You fear nothing more than courage.
You who turn away your eyes
At the bravery of the young men.

You,
The hyena with polished face and bow tie,
In the office of a billion dollar
Corporation devoted to service;
The vulture dripping with carrion,
Carefully and carelessly robed in imported tweeds,
Lecturing on the Age of Abundance;
The jackal in double-breasted gabardine,

Barking by remote control,
In the United Nations;
The vampire bat seated at the couch head,
Notebook in hand, toying with his decerebrator;
The autonomous, ambulatory cancer,
The Superego in a thousand uniforms;
You, the finger man of behemoth,
The murderer of the young men.

II

What happened to Robinson,
Who used to stagger down Eighth Street,
Dizzy with solitary gin?
Where is Masters, who crouched in
His law office for ruinous decades?
Where is Leonard who thought he was
A locomotive? And Lindsay,
Wise as a dove, innocent
As a serpent, where is he?
      Timor mortis conturbat me.

What became of Jim Oppenheim?
Lola Ridge alone in an
Icy furnished room? Orrick Johns,
Hopping into the surf on his
One leg? Elinor Wylie
Who leaped like Kierkegaard?
Sara Teasdale, where is she?
      Timor mortis conturbat me.

Where is George Sterling, that tame fawn?
Phelps Putnam who stole away?
Jack Wheelwright who couldn't cross the bridge?
Donald Evans with his cane and
Monocle, where is he?
      Timor mortis conturbat me.

John Gould Fletcher who could not
Unbreak his powerful heart?
Bodenheim butchered in stinking
Squalor? Edna Millay who took
Her last straight whiskey? Genevieve
Who loved so much; where is she?
    Timor mortis conturbat me.

Harry who didn't care at all?
Hart who went back to the sea?
    Timor mortis conturbat me.

Where is Sol Funaroff?
What happened to Potamkin?
Isidor Schneider? Claude McKay?
Countee Cullen? Clarence Weinstock?
Who animates their corpses today?
    Timor mortis conturbat me.

Where is Ezra, that noisy man?
Where is Larsson whose poems were prayers?
Where is Charles Snider, that gentle
Bitter boy? Carnevali,
What became of him?
Carol who was so beautiful, where is she?
    Timor mortis conturbat me.

    III

Was their end noble and tragic,
Like the mask of a tyrant?
Like Agamemnon's secret golden face?
Indeed it was not. Up all night
In the fo'c'sle, bemused and beaten,
Bleeding at the rectum, in his
Pocket a review by the one
Colleague he respected, "If he
Really means what these poems
Pretend to say, he has only

One way out —." Into the
Hot acrid Caribbean sun,
Into the acrid, transparent,
Smoky sea. Or another, lice in his
Armpits and crotch, garbage littered
On the floor, gray greasy rags on
The bed. "I killed them because they
Were dirty, stinking Communists.
I should get a medal." Again,
Another, Simenon foretold,
His end at a glance. "I dare you
To pull the trigger." She shut her eyes
And spilled gin over her dress.
The pistol wobbled in his hand.
It took them hours to die.
Another threw herself downstairs,
And broke her back. It took her years.
Two put their heads under water
In the bath and filled their lungs.
Another threw himself under
The traffic of a crowded bridge.
Another, drunk, jumped from a
Balcony and broke her neck.
Another soaked herself in
Gasoline and ran blazing
Into the street and lived on
In custody. One made love
Only once with a beggar woman.
He died years later of syphilis
Of the brain and spine. Fifteen
Years of pain and poverty,
While his mind leaked away.
One tried three times in twenty years
To drown himself. The last time
He succeeded. One turned on the gas
When she had no more food, no more
Money, and only half a lung.
One went up to Harlem, took on
Thirty men, came home and
Cut her throat. One sat up all night

Talking to H. L. Mencken and
Drowned himself in the morning.
How many stopped writing at thirty?
How many went to work for *Time?*
How many died of prefrontal
Lobotomies in the Communist Party?
How many are lost in the back wards
Of provincial madhouses?
How many on the advice of
Their psychoanalysts, decided
A business career was best after all?
How many are hopeless alcoholics?
René Crevel!
Jacques Rigaud!
Antonin Artaud!
Mayakofsky!
Essenin!
Robert Desnos!
Saint Pol Roux!
Max Jacob!
All over the world
The same disembodied hand
Strikes us down.
Here is a mountain of death.
A hill of heads like the Khans piled up.
The first-born of a century
Slaughtered by Herod.
Three generations of infants
Stuffed down the maw of Moloch.

        IV

He is dead.
The bird of Rhiannon.
He is dead.
In the winter of the heart.
He is Dead.
In the canyons of death,
They found him dumb at last,

In the blizzard of lies.
He never spoke again.
He died.
He is dead.
In their antiseptic hands,
He is dead.
The little spellbinder of Cader Idris.
He is dead.
The sparrow of Cardiff.
He is dead.
The canary of Swansea.
Who killed him?
Who killed the bright-headed bird?
You did, you son of a bitch.
You drowned him in your cocktail brain.
He fell down and died in your synthetic heart.
You killed him,
Oppenheimer the Million-Killer,
You killed him,
Einstein the Gray Eminence.
You killed him,
Havanahavana, with your Nobel Prize.
You killed him, General,
Through the proper channels.
You strangled him, Le Mouton,
With your *mains étendues*.
He confessed in open court to a pince-nezed skull.
You shot him in the back of the head
As he stumbled in the last cellar.
You killed him,
Benign Lady on the postage stamp.
He was found dead at a Liberal Weekly luncheon.
He was found dead on the cutting room floor.
He was found dead at a *Time* policy conference.
Henry Luce killed him with a telegram to the Pope.
Mademoiselle strangled him with a padded brassiere.
Old Possum sprinkled him with a tea ball.
After the wolves were done, the vaticides
Crawled off with his bowels to their classrooms
    and quarterlies.
When the news came over the radio

You personally rose up shouting, "Give us Barabbas!"
In your lonely crowd you swept over him.
Your custom-built brogans and your ballet slippers
Pummeled him to death in the gritty street.
You hit him with an album of Hindemith.
You stabbed him with stainless steel by Isamu Noguchi,
He is dead.
He is Dead.
Like Ignacio the bullfighter,
At four o'clock in the afternoon.
At precisely four o'clock.
I too do not want to hear it.
I too do not want to know it.
I want to run into the street,
Shouting, "Remember Vanzetti!"
I want to pour gasoline down your chimneys.
I want to blow up your galleries.
I want to burn down your editorial offices.
I want to slit the bellies of your frigid women.
I want to sink your sailboats and launches.
I want to strangle your children at their finger paintings.
I want to poison your Afghans and poodles.
He is dead, the little drunken cherub.
He is dead,
The effulgent tub thumper.
He is Dead.
The ever living birds are not singing
To the head of Bran.
The sea birds are still
Over Bardsey of Ten Thousand Saints.
The underground men are not singing
On their way to work.
There is a smell of blood
In the smell of the turf smoke.
They have struck him down,
The son of David ap Gwilym.
They have murdered him,
The Baby of Taliessin.
There he lies dead,

By the Iceberg of the United Nations.
There he lies sandbagged,
At the foot of the Statue of Liberty.
The Gulf Stream smells of blood
As it breaks on the sand of Iona
And the blue rocks of Canarvon.
And all the birds of the deep sea rise up
Over the luxury liners and scream,
"You killed him! You killed him.
In your God damned Brooks Brothers suit,
You son of a bitch."

from A BESTIARY

for my daughters, Mary and Katharine

Aardvark

The man who found the aardvark
Was laughed out of the meeting
Of the Dutch Academy.
Nobody would believe him.
The aardvark had its revenge —
It returned in dreams, in smoke,
In anonymous letters.
One day somebody found out
It was in Hieronymus
Bosch all the time. From there it
Had sneaked off to Africa.

Cat

There are too many poems
About cats. Beware of cat
Lovers, they have a hidden
Frustration somewhere and will
Stick you with it if they can.

Fox

The fox is very clever.
In England people dress up
Like a movie star's servants
And chase the fox on horses.
Rather, they let dogs chase him,
And they come along behind.
When the dogs have torn the fox
To pieces they rub his blood
On the faces of young girls.
If you are clever do not
Let anybody know it,
But especially Englishmen.

Goat

G stands for goat and also
For genius. If you are one,
Learn from the other, for he
Combines domestication,
Venery, and independence.

Herring

The herring is prolific.
There are plenty of herrings.
Some herrings are eaten raw.
Many are dried and pickled.
But most are used for manure.
See if you can apply this
To your history lessons.

I

Take care of this. It's all there is.
You will never get another.

Lion

The lion is called the king
Of beasts. Nowadays there are
Almost as many lions
In cages as out of them.
If offered a crown, refuse.

Man

Someday, if you are lucky,
You'll each have one for your own.
Try it before you pick it.
Some kinds are made of soybeans.
Give it lots to eat and sleep.
Treat it nicely and it will
Always do just what you want.

Raccoon

The raccoon wears a black mask,
And he washes everything
Before he eats it. If you
Give him a cube of sugar,
He'll wash it away and weep.
Some of life's sweetest pleasures
Can be enjoyed only if
You don't mind a little dirt.
Here a false face won't help you.

Uncle Sam

Like the unicorn, Uncle
Sam is what is called a myth.
Plato wrote a book which is
An occult conspiracy
Of gentlemen pederasts.
In it he said ideas

Are more nobly real than
Reality, and that myths
Help keep people in their place.
Since you will never become,
Under any circumstances,
Gentlemen pederasts, you'd
Best leave these blood-soaked notions
To those who find them useful.

Unicorn

The unicorn is supposed
To seek a virgin, lay
His head in her lap, and weep,
Whereupon she steals his horn.
Virginity is what is
Known as a privation. It is
Very difficult to find
Any justification for
Something that doesn't exist.
However, in your young days
You might meet a unicorn.
There are not many better
Things than a unicorn horn.

Vulture

St. Thomas Aquinas thought
That vultures were lesbians
And fertilized by the wind.
If you seek the facts of life,
Papist intellectuals
Can be very misleading.

Wolf

Never believe all you hear.
Wolves are not as bad as lambs.
I've been a wolf all my life,
And have two lovely daughters
To show for it, while I could
Tell you sickening tales of
Lambs who got their just deserts.

from NATURAL NUMBERS (1964)

FISH PEDDLER AND COBBLER

Always for thirty years now
I am in the mountains in
August. For thirty Augusts
Your ghosts have stood up over
The mountains. That was nineteen
Twenty seven. Now it is
Nineteen fifty seven. Once
More after thirty years I
Am back in the mountains of
Youth, back in the Gros Ventres,
The broad park-like valleys and
The tremendous cubical
Peaks of the Rockies. I learned
To shave hereabouts, working
As cookee and night wrangler.
Nineteen twenty two, the years
Of revolutionary
Hope that came to an end as
The iron fist began to close.
No one electrocuted me.
Nothing happened. Time passed.
Something invisible was gone.
We thought then that we were the men
Of the years of the great change,
That we were the forerunners
Of the normal life of mankind.
We thought that soon all things would
Be changed, not just economic
And social relationships, but
Painting, poetry, music, dance,
Architecture, even the food
We ate and the clothes we wore
Would be ennobled. It will take
Longer than we expected.

These mountains are unchanged since
I was a boy wandering
Over the West, picking up
Odd jobs. If anything they are
Wilder. A moose cow blunders
Into camp. Beavers slap their tails
On their sedgy pond as we fish
From on top of their lodge in the
Twilight. The horses feed on bright grass
In meadows full of purple gentian,
And stumble through silver dew
In the full moonlight.
The fish taste of meadow water.
In the morning on far grass ridges
Above the red rim rock wild sheep
Bound like rubber balls over the
Horizon as the noise of camp
Begins. I catch and saddle
Mary's little golden horse,
And pack the first Decker saddles
I've seen in thirty years. Even
The horse bells have a different sound
From the ones in California.
Canada jays fight over
The last scraps of our pancakes.
On the long sandy pass we ride
Through fields of lavender primrose
While lightning explodes around us.
For lunch Mary catches a two pound
Grayling in the whispering river.
No fourteen thousand foot peaks
Are named Sacco and Vanzetti.
Not yet. The clothes I wear
Are as unchanged as the Decker
Saddles on the pack horses.
America grows rich on the threat of death.
Nobody bothers anarchists anymore.
Coming back we lay over
In Ogden for ten hours.
The courthouse square was full

Of miners and lumberjacks and
Harvest hands and gandy dancers
With broken hands and broken
Faces sleeping off cheap wine drunks
In the scorching heat, while tired
Savage eyed whores paraded the street.

from WRITTEN TO MUSIC

Married Blues

I didn't want it, you wanted it.
Now you've got it you don't like it.
You can't get out of it now.

Pork and beans, diapers to wash,
Too poor for the movies, too tired to love.
There's nothing we can do.

Hot stenographers on the subway.
The grocery boy's got a big one.
We can't do anything about it.

You're only young once.
You've got to go when your time comes.
That's how it is. Nobody can change it.

Guys in big cars whistle.
Freight trains moan in the night.
We can't get away with it.

That's the way life is.
Everybody's in the same fix.
It will never be any different.

from THE HEART'S GARDEN,
THE GARDEN'S HEART (1967)

II

Pausing in my sixth decade
At the end of a journey
Around the earth—where am I?
I am sitting on a rock
Close beside a waterfall
Above Kurama Hot Springs
In the hills above Kyoto.
So I have sat by hundreds,
In the Adirondacks and
The Green Mountains of Vermont,
In the Massif Central, Alps,
Cascades, Rockies, Sierras,
Even Niagara long, long
Ago in a night of snow.
The water speaks the same language.
It should have told me something
All these years, all these places,
Always saying the same thing.
I should have learned more than I did,
My wit ought to have been more.
I am now older than I was,
In Winters and in lore.
What can I see before me
In the water's smoke and mist?
I should have learned something. "Who
Am I? What can I do? What can I
Hope?" Kant on Euler's bridges
Of dilemma in Koenigsberg.
Somewhere in some topology
The knots untie themselves,
The bridges are all connected.
Is that true? How do you know?
"What is love?" said jesting Pilate
And would not stay for an answer.

I have asked many idle
Questions since the day I could speak.
Now I have many Winters
But very few answers.
Age has me bestolen on
Ere I it wist.
Ne might I see before me
For smoke nor for mist. The smoke
And mist of the waterfall
Shifts and billows. The double
Rainbow remains constant.
There are more years behind me
Than years ahead, and have been
For a very long time. What
Remains in either pan of
The unstable balances of time?
Childbirth, love, and ecstasy
Activate nerves otherwise
Never used and so are hard
To recall, and visions are
The measure of the defect
Of vision. I loved. I saw.
All the way down to Kyoto,
And high above me on all
The ridges are temples full of
Buddhas. This village of stone
Carvers and woodcutters is
Its own illimitable Buddha world.
The illuminated live
Always in light and so do
Not know it is there as fishes
Do not know they live in water.
Under the giant cypresses
Amongst the mossy stones and
Bamboo grass there are white stars
Of dwarf iris everywhere.
The forest is filled with incense.
Boys' Day, the giant wind carp
Float in the breeze of early
Summer over all the houses

Of this mountain village.
The light, cheap, paper ones do.
The more durable cloth ones
Hardly lift and sway at all.
There are rocks on the earth
More durable than the
Constellations of heaven.
Gold leaves of feather bamboo
Fall through the warm wind of May
On to the white rectangle
Of raked gravel in the temple
Garden. Why does the bamboo shed
Its leaves at this time of year?
Smoky, oppressively hot,
The evening comes to an end.
An uguisu sings in the gnarled pine.
The cuckoos call in the ginko trees,
Just like they do in the old poems.
Swallows mate on the telephone wires.
A wood pigeon, speckled like
A quail, drinks from the dew basin.
The new leaves are just coming in.
The bamboos look like green gold smoke.
In the weavers' quarter
Beyond the temple walls,
As the noises of the day cease
I can hear the throb and clack
Of thousands of home looms.
Nishikigi—but no ghosts rise.
Gold fish swim in the moat, red
As fire, they burn in the brown
Water. The moat guards the scriptures
From fire, but the Buddha word
Is burning like the dry grass on
The Indian hills and like the stars.
How easy it is for men
To do right—the submarine
Green of young maple leaves on moss,
Fourteen trees and some earth bare
Of all but moss, and the light

Like Cours Mirabeau in Aix
Before greed destroyed it.
The turtle is the symbol
Of obscenity, but all
The moats that guard the scriptures
Are planted with honorable
Turtles. Turtle-san, protect
The Three Jewels, as the lewd
Pigeons in the air protect
The Great Void. When they rut and beg
In the gravel garden, they fill
Their craws with uncut stones.
"Vectors of reticulation."
We are defined by the webs
Of ten thousand lines of force.
Rocks surrounded by currents
Of raked gravel. Stripes of tigers
Playing in the bamboo shade.
Lichens on ruined dragon stones.
"When I see the wild chrysanthemum
Blooming in the crannies
Of the cliff, I try to forget
The glories of the capital."
The water ouzel walks on
The bottom under the torrent
And builds her nest behind the
Waterfall. Kurama River,
Kaweah River, it is
The same water ouzel although
It is a different species.

VI

The Eve of Ch'ing Ming—Clear Bright,
A quail's breast sky and smoky hills,
The great bronze gong booms in the
Russet sunset. Late tonight

It will rain. Tomorrow will
Be clear and cool once more. One more
Clear, bright day in this floating life.
The slopes of Mt. Hiei are veiled
In haze for the last day of Spring.
Spring mist turns to Summer haze
And hides the distant mountains,
But the first evening breeze
Brings the scent of their flowers.
I say a few words and the haze
Lifts from Mt. Hiei and trees
And temples and climbing people
Stand out as sharp as glass.
Three red pigeons on the sunbaked
Gravel, murmuring like the
Far off voices of people
I loved once. The turtles sleep
On the surface of the moat.
If belief and anxiety,
Covetousness and grasping,
Be banished from experience
Of any object whatever,
Only its essence remains,
Only its ultimate being.
He who lives without grasping
Lives always in experience
Of the immediate as the
Ultimate. The solution
Of the problem of knowing
And being is ethical.
Epistemology is moral.
The rutting cock pigeons fill
Their craws with cob from the wall.
Each has his territory,
Where, already this season,
He has dug a hole as big
As a tea cup. They defend
The holes against intrusion
Like they quarrel over the hens.
The knot tied without a rope

Cannot be untied. The seven
Bridges of Koenigsberg cannot
Be crossed but you can always
Go for a swim in the river.
The lower leaves of the trees
Tangle the sunset in dusk.
Awe perfumes the warm twilight.
St. John of the Cross said it,
The desire for vision is
The sin of gluttony.
The bush warbler sings in the
Ancient white pine by the temple
Of the Buddha of Healing.

X

The sound of gongs, the songs of birds,
The chanting of men, floating wisps
Of incense, drifting pine smoke,
Perfume of the death of Spring—
The warm breeze clouds the mirror
With the pollen of the pines,
And thrums the strings of the lute.
Higher in the mountains the
Wild cherry is still blooming.
The driving mist tears away
And scatters the last petals,
And tears the human heart. Altair
and Vega climb to the zenith.
A long whistling wail on the flute,
The drummer makes a strangling cry.
And to the clacking of the sticks,
The weaving girl dances for
Her cowboy far across the
Cloudy River. Wings waver
And break. Pine boughs sigh in the
Dark. The water of life runs
Quick through dry reeds.

Under the full moon, a piercing
Fragrance spreads through the white night
Like the perfume of new snow.
An unknown tree has blossomed
Outside my cabin window.
In the warm night cold air drains
Down the mountain stream and fills
The summer valley with the
Incense of early Spring. I
Remember a grass hut on
A rainy night, dreaming of
The past, and my tears starting
At the cry of a mountain cuckoo.
Her bracelets tinkle, her anklets
Clink. She sways at her clattering
Loom. She hurries to have a new
Obi ready when he comes—
On the seventh day of the seventh
Month when the pachinko balls
Fall like meteor swarms.
   Click clack click click clack click
Cho Cho
   Click clack click click clack click
Cho Cho
   Toak. tolk. tock. toak. toik. tok. tok.
Chidori. Chidori.
Kannon. Kannon.
The great hawk went down the river
In the twilight. The belling owl
Went up the river in the
Moonlight. He returns to
Penelope, the wanderer
Of many devices, to
The final woman who weaves,
And unweaves, and weaves again.
In the moon drenched night the floating
Bridge of dreams breaks off. The clouds
Banked against the mountain peak
Dissipate in the clear sky.

from NEW POEMS (1974)

Now the starlit moonless Spring

Now the starlit moonless Spring
Night stands over the Fontaine
De Medicis, and the gold
Fish swim in the cold, starlit
Water. Yesterday, in the
New sunshine, lovers sat by
The water, and talked, and fed
The goldfish, and kissed each other.
I am in California
And evening is coming on.
Now it is morning in Paris
By the Fontaine de Medicis.
And the lovers will come today,
And talk and kiss, and feed the fish,
After they have had their coffee.

I DREAM OF LESLIE

You entered my sleep,
Come with your immense,
Luminous eyes,
And light brown hair,
Across fifty years,
To sing for me again that song
Of Campion's we loved so once.
I kissed your quivering throat.
There was no hint in the dream
That you were long, long since
A new arrivéd guest,
With blithe Helen, white Iope and the rest—
Only the peace
Of late afternoon

In a compassionate autumn
In youth.
And I forgot
That I was old and you a shade.

LA VIE EN ROSE

Fog fills the little square
Between Avenue du Maine
And the Gaité Montparnasse.
I walk around and around,
Waiting for my girl.
My footsteps echo
From the walls
Of the second storeys.
Deep in the future
My ghost follows me,
Around and around.

SUCHNESS

In the theosophy of light,
The logical universal
Ceases to be anything more
Than the dead body of an angel.
What is substance? Our substance
Is whatever we feed our angel.
The perfect incense for worship
Is camphor, whose flames leave no ashes.

from ON FLOWER WREATH HILL (1976)

I

An aging pilgrim on a
Darkening path walks through the
Fallen and falling leaves, through
A forest grown over the
Hilltop tumulus of a
Long dead princess, as the
Moonlight grows and the daylight
Fades and the Western Hills turn
Dim in the distance and the
Lights come on, pale green
In the streets of the hazy city.

I V

No leaf stirs. I am alone
In the midst of a hundred
Empty mountains. Cicadas,
Locusts, katydids, crickets,
Have fallen still, one after
Another. Even the wind
Bells hang motionless. In the
Blue dusk, widely spaced snowflakes
Fall in perfect verticals.
Yet, under my cabin porch,
The thin, clear Autumn water
Rustles softly like fine silk.

V

This world of ours, before we
Can know its fleeting sorrows,
We enter it through tears.
Do the reverberations
Of the evening bell of
The mountain temple ever
Totally die away?
Memory echoes and reechoes
Always reinforcing itself.
No wave motion ever dies.
The white waves of the wake of
The boat that rows away into
The dawn, spread and lap on the
Sands of the shores of all the world.

from THE SILVER SWAN (1978)

I V

Under the half moon
The field crickets are silent.
Only the cricket
Of the hearth still sings, louder
Still, behind the gas heater.

X I V

Hototogisu—horobirete

The cuckoo's call, though
Sweet in itself, is hard to
Bear, for it cries,
"Perishing! Perishing!"
Against the Spring.

X I X

The drowned moon plunges
Through a towering surf
Of storm clouds, and momently
The wet leaves glitter.
Moment by moment an owl cries.
Rodents scurry, building
Their winter nests, in the moments of dark.

from THE LOVE POEMS OF MARICHIKO
(1978)

VII

Making love with you
Is like drinking sea water.
The more I drink
The thirstier I become,
Until nothing can slake my thirst
But to drink the entire sea.

IX

You wake me,
Part my thighs, and kiss me.
I give you the dew
Of the first morning of the world.

XXV

Your tongue thrums and moves
Into me, and I become
Hollow and blaze with
Whirling light, like the inside
Of a vast expanding pearl.

XXVII

As I came from the
Hot bath, you took me before

The horizontal mirror
Beside the low bed, while my
Breasts quivered in your hands, my
Buttocks shivered against you.

XXXI

Some day in six inches of
Ashes will be all
That's left of our passionate minds,
Of all the world created
By our love, its origin
And passing away.

XXXII

I hold your head tight between
My thighs, and press against your
Mouth, and float away
Forever, in an orchid
Boat on the River of Heaven.

XXXIII

I cannot forget
The perfumed dusk inside the
Tent of my black hair,
As we awoke to make love
After a long night of love.

from THE HOMESTEAD CALLED DAMASCUS
(1920–1925)

I

Heaven is full of definite stars
And crowded with modest angels, robed
In tubular, neuter folds of pink and blue.
Their feet tread doubtless on that utter
Hollowness, with never a question
Of the "ineluctable modality"
Of the invisible; busy, orderly,
Content to ignore the coal pockets
In the galaxy, dark nebulae,
And black broken windows into space.
Youthful minds may fret infinity,
Moistly dishevelled, poking in odd
Corners for unsampled vocations
Of the spirit, while the flesh is strong.
Experience sinks its roots in space—
Euclidean, warped, or otherwise.
The will constructs rhomboids, nonagons,
And paragons in time to suit each taste.
Or, if not the will, then circumstance.
History demands satisfaction,
And never lacks, with or without help
From the subjects of its curious science.

Thomas Damascan and the mansion,
A rambling house with Doric columns
On the upper Hudson in the Catskills,
Called Damascus. We were walking there
Once in early Spring; his brother Sebastian
Said, staring into the underbrush,
"If you'll look close you'll see the panthers
In there eating the crocus." And Thomas said,
"Panthers are always getting into
The crocus. Every spring. There were too many
Panthers about the courts in my father's time."

They had an odd wry sort of family humor
That startled idle minds and plagued your
Memory for years afterwards.
We sat up late that night drinking wine,
Playing chess, arguing—Plato and Leibnitz,
Einstein, Freud and Marx, and woke at noon.
The next day was grey and rained till twilight,
And ice from somewhere in the Adirondacks
Drifted soggily down the river.
In the afternoon Sebastian read
The Golden Bough, and Thomas said,
"Remember, in school, after we read Frazer,
I insisted on signing myself Tammuz,
To the horror of all our teachers?"
"And now," he said, "We're middle aged, wise,"
(They were very far from middle aged.)
"And what we thought once was irony
Is simple fact, simple, sensuous,
And so forth. Fate is a poor scholar."
We said nothing, and the three of us
Watched the rain fall through the budding trees,
Until at last Thomas rose and took
A bow from the rack, sprung it, and said,
"I wish we could shoot these things in the rain."
Sebastian said, "I'd much rather shoot
In the sunshine, and besides it spoils
The arrows. I'm going for a hike."
So we went off through the hanging woods,
Single file, and up the steep meadow,
Scratched by thistles, in a thistle wind—
Last year's thistles, and a pungent wind.
Thomas said, "We've got to move the goats
Before they ruin all the pasture.
There'll be nothing but thistles next year."
Sebastian said, "Thistles or blue grass,
Goats or cattle, what does it matter,
We'll have to die quick to be buried here."
The goats hurried ahead up the slope,
Stopped among the rocks and there gave us
Their clinical goatish regard.

We climbed to the top of the Pope's Nose
And stood looking out at the river,
Slaty in the rain, and the traffic
Wallowing on the muddy highway,
And beneath us in the closed hollow,
The swollen carp ponds, the black water
Flowing through the clattering rushes,
And, poised each on one cold leg, two herons,
Staring over their puckered shoulders
At a hieroglyph of crows in the distance.

. . . .

II

THE AUTUMN OF MANY YEARS

. . . .

How short a time for a life to last.
So few years, so narrow a space, so
Slight a melody, a handful of
Notes. Most of it dreams and dreamless sleep,
And solitary walks in empty
Parks and foggy streets. Or all alone,
In the midst of nightstruck, excited
Crowds. Once in a while one of them
Spoke, or a face smiled, but not often.
One or two could recall the tune if asked.
Now she is gone. Hooded candles in
The Spring wind tilt and move down the
Narrow columned aisle. Incense plumes whirl.
Thuribles clink. The last smoke dissolves
Above the rain soaked hills, the black pines,
Broken by a flock of migrating birds.

Thomas climbed the ice and crossed the pass.
Coneys whistled in the shrill air. Ice
And rock and indigo sky—Enoch
Walked the hills and waged war on substance

In the vertical. Is it best to
Remember always the same memory,
To see the world always in the same hour?
Good Friday, incense and hooded candles.
Sebastian descends the wet hillside
Into the coiling river fog. He
Sinks from sight into the hidden world.
And on the mountain crest the tattered
Crows wheel like an apparition
In a fog as serpentine and cold,
And much more opaque, and unseen caw
And caw. This hour the sacramental
Man was broken on the height, in dark
Opacity rent with caw and caw.

Thomas, called Tammuz, the first
Of twins, "the beloved one," the one
Called Didymus in the upper room—
The involuntary active man—
Peers in the black wounds, hammers the frame
That squeezes the will. The arrow breaks.
He breaks the gold arrow in the gold
Light. The arrow breaks the brittle flesh,
Breaking upon it. Baldur in the
Autumn, the image of the twin.
The Autumn light, the level lawn.
Modred, Iscariot, Loki cross
Beyond the Catskills. Sebastian drinks
Cold astringent tea in the damp
Summer house above the hazy river.

III

THE DOUBLE HELLAS

Claret enim claris quod clare concopulator

. . . .

The world is composed of a pair of
Broken pillars, a round sun in a

Rigid sky, a sea, and in the great
Distance, a red line of cliffs. The world
Is composed of a pair of broken
Pillars, of pillars, of a suave line
Conceived in a mind infinitely
Refined by edges infinitely
Sharp. The world is composed. There is a
Little boat upon the sea, a striped
Sail. They raise a net from the bright sea
And go away rowing with the wind.
Recently awe and precision hung
In this landscape, the keen edge of pride,
The suave line, the Doric mind. Voices
Of children come up the steep valley.
A blur of smoke smudges the skyline.
"Come back, baby, I miss your little
Brown body and your childish ways."
"Hush, Chloris, heed not the stars
Narcissistically parading
There above the mannered pools."
You can always find pity
And terror amongst the broken
Statuary. Whose profiles
Coin the wind? The Bactrian
Kings. Pisanello's courtesans.
The whole sky is made of gold.
The dancing master in a
Castled wig, Priapus in
The vines. The soft sliding eyes.
"Ah, Chloris, heed not the stars,
The smoky shattering fountains
In the teeming night."

My parents had their life, it was not
Your soft dark tragedy. It was not
Anything like it. Saffron twilights
Over the gas lit horse drawn city.
Purple and gold above the desert.
When they were sad, they shut their mouths tight.
When God spoke to Job from the whirlwind

128

He refused to answer his questions—
On the advice of his attorney.
The rainbow mountains glitter in
The breaking prism. Within the mirror
Of ice, pain speaks to sorrow outside.
And now the sun has set and the strange
Blake-like forms fade from our memories.
The sky was deeper than a ruby.
The hoarfrost spreads over the marshes
Like a mandolin note over water.
Between the mountains a candle burned.
A narrow leaf of flame casting no
Light about it. The epic hero
Came, in full armor, making a huge
Clatter, and fell, struck down from behind,
And lay in the barren eternal
Dawn, geometrically prostrate,
As the clock ticks measured out his death—
As the spouting flame leaped from roof to
Roof and all the houses full of ticking
Clocks caught fire one after another.

. . . .

IV

THE STIGMATA OF FACT

. . . .

Morphology repeats ontology.
Thomas drank all night and read John of the Cross.
He was drunk and forsaken before
Dawn. At daylight he went out through the
Lion Gate and bought a ticket for
Knossos, where the women paint their breasts
And the men use perfume and the girls
Mate with bulls. The crowd boiled around him,
Lonely as beasts in a slaughter house.
The period grew blackly backward
Across its sentence. Theseus died

At last in a vulgar brawl. The priests,
Stinking of perfume, got him ready.
Why these overstained contortionist
Tricks? Archaeologists have proved
The Minotaur a lie, the labyrinth
A vast grocery store, Knossos so mild
It went unwalled. Even the Easter
Island anthropoliths were harmless
Statues of the royal kinfolks. Near
To us, nearer than the lamps that lit
The ceilings of Altamira and Dordogne,
The uncanny geomorphous companions wait—
Maybe, but today his theromorphs
Have outlasted every Pharaoh.

Saturday night, rain falls in the slums.
Rain veils the tired hurrying faces,
Sordid and beautiful in the rain.
Sebastian walks, puzzled, in the rain.
This is the macrocosm, on these
Materials it subsists. And the
Microcosm—This is the very thing.
There is no self that suffers rebirth.
Few trigliths of Stonehenge still stand there
In that immense windy nightbound plain.
It is cold after the summer rain.
"This is the place," she says, "Let's eat here."
She turns against him, warm and firm, rain
On her brown cheeks and odorous hair.
When he got home his cheeks were bronze, too,
As though with fever rather than sun,
His beard grizzled, his hair thinner.
The old dog discovered him and died.
The evil rivals died. The web flew wide.
And this was the little brother, the
Holy comedian, offering
Him the password at which all rusted
Hinges fall. This is the place where knowledge
Was so close to poplars and to stones.

Thomas looks out over the valley.
Far off in the low mists and fireflies
The lights along the railroad track change.
Then the whistle comes as distant as
A star and finally the distant
Roar and like a diamond necklace falling
Through the long somber valley the lighted
Cars, pulsating and slipping away
And the headlight twisting into the
Dimness like a cold needle. All so
Far away, not like a toy train but
Like some bright micro organism,
The night train to Omaha goes by.
Then Thomas quiets the zebra dun,
Tends the bannock and the tea and turns
The bacon. Grey low shapes of night bulk
Slow and make their own horizon. White
Ash flakes fall from the heart of the fire.
Now far, now near, the chuck-will's-widows
Call. Thomas smokes and spits into the
Fire. Bats cry, the creaking of the hundred,
Tiny, closing doors of silence.

from A PROLEGOMENON TO A THEODICY*
(1925–1927)

II

We were interested in ways of being
We saw lives
We saw animals
We saw agile rodents
Scala rodent
The harmonic pencil
Scala rodent
Emits its fundamental
The stricken plethora
A bottle of water against a very blue sky
A toppling shutter
The final peninsulas of space
Germinate in the secret ovoid perimeter
e.g.: scholia
The white hill
Elastic fatigue
The white lax hill and immediately the iced antelope
The line warps
The meridian of least resistance ascends the sky
The brain ferments
The curdled brain
The repercussion
The bullweaver
Obsessed by an ideograph
A mechanical bracelet
A small diesel engine
First one and then the other
Air congeals in water
The mural rift
A kind of going

---

*A long excerpt from this poem was originally published in *An "Objectivists" Anthology* (Le Beausset: To Publishers, 1932).

The little block falls
The little wooden block
That long snarl of coast on the Mediterranean
The heart inclines
The four triangles
The fifth
The fingers jerk
The green cheek
The fourth
The image in the portal
The resin curls
The soggy mitten
The third
The cleaved cough
The second
The closing ribs
The first
The double envoi
The grackle breaks
Sweat
The diverse arrows
The anagogic eye

III

This is the winter of the hardest year
And did you dream
The white the large
The slow movement
The type of dream
The terror
The stumble stone
The winter the snow that was there
The neck and the hand
The head
The snow that was in the air
The long sun
The exodus of thought
The enervated violin

The oiled temples
The singing song and the sung
The lengthy home
The trundling endless stairs
The young stone
Homing and the song
The air that was there
Flayed jaws piled on the steps
The twirling rain
And laying they repeat the horizon
Ineffably to know how it goes swollen and then not swollen
Cold and then too warm
So many minor electrocutions
So many slaps of nausea
The keen eyelids
The abrupt diastole
That leaves you wondering
Why it was ever despite their assurances unlocked
Stars like lice along the scalp
The brain pan bitten burning
And dull on one foot
And dull on one foot
O cry aloud
O teeth unbound
Don't you know that the stone walk alone
Do you know the shredded brow
Are you aware
Do you take this forever concentric bland freezing to touch
Let the scarlet rustle
Let the globes come down
Let the oblate spheroids fall infinitely away
Forever away always falling but you can always see them
The creak
The squeak that makes you so slightly open your mouth
Patiently to be strangled
It is gone away somewhere
It is Winter
Reason
Winter
Ache

IX

a

The bell
Too softly and too slowly tolled
And the first wave was snow
The second ice
The third fire
The fourth blood
The fifth adders
The sixth smother
The seventh foul stink
And unnumbered beasts swam in the sea
Some feather footed
Some devoid of any feet
And all with fiery eyes
And phosphorescent breath
The enduring bell
The wash of wave
The wiry cranes that stagger in the air
The hooded eyes struggling in the confused littoral
The smoky cloak
Those who walk
Those who are constrained
Those who watch the hole of wavering dark
There is no order in expectation
The feet fall
Even the enemy of cold labor
Of the mighty tongue
The gull matted on the sand
Worms spilling out of the beak
The cervical agony
Unplumbed and unforgotten caves
A cry sent up in expectation
A mouth filling the sky
Shaping the words of the victor
The bell
A voice
Blessed are the dead who die
The generations of generations

b

They were in an unstable condition
Floating about in a putrid fog
Throughout the tangled forest
Between the charred trunks
Over the yellow marshes
Some squirmed after the manner of lizards
Some were upright with their arms held up
Some lay with their knees partly drawn up
Some lay on their sides
Some lay stretched at full length
Some lay on their backs
Some were stooping
Some held their heads bent down
Some drew up their legs
Some embraced
Some kicked out with arms and legs
Some were kneeling
Some stood and inhaled deep breaths
Some crawled
Some walked
Some felt about in the dark
Some arose
Some gazed, sitting still

d

Light
Light
The sliver in the firmament
The stirring horde
The rocking wave
The name breaks in the sky
Why stand we
Why go we nought
They broken seek the cleaving balance
The young men gone
Lux lucis
The revolving company

The water flowing from the right side
Et fons luminis
The ciborium of the abyss
The bread of light
The chalice of the byss
The wine of flaming light
The wheeling multitude
The rocking cry
The reverberant scalar song lifts up
The metric finger aeon by aeon
And the cloud of memory descends
The regnant fruitful vine
The exploding rock
The exploding mountain cry
Tris agios
The sapphire snow
Hryca hryca nazaza

NOTES

The following notes are intended as a guide to some of the more difficult references in the poems included in this volume and not as comprehensive commentary.

from IN WHAT HOUR (1940)

August 22, 1939
Nicola Sacco: Nicola Sacco and Bartolomeo Vanzetti, both immigrants and radicals, were arrested for robbery and the murder of two employees of a shoe factory in South Braintree, Massachusetts, in April 1920. Their conviction stirred a public outcry joined by many prominent writers and intellectuals. They were executed on August 23, 1937.

Angst und Gestalt und Gebet: The last line of the poem "Erinnerung" ("Remembering") by Rainer Marie Rilke (1875–1926) translates from the German, "Anguish and form and prayer."

Pisgah: Mountain at the northern end of the Dead Sea (highest elevation, 2,644 ft.) from which Moses viewed the promised land but could not enter (Deut. 3:27, 4:29).

"From each according to . . . need": Karl Marx, *Critique of the Gotha Program*, I.

Kropotkin: Pyotr Kropotkin (1842–1921), Russian revolutionary, a leader and theorist of the anarchist movement, died disenchanted with the Bolsheviks.

Berkman: Alexander Berkman (1870–1936), American anarchist, who attempted to assassinate Henry Clay Frick. Eventually he was deported in 1919 with Emma Goldman for agitation against conscription and traveled to Russia, but left in 1921 disillusioned with the Bolshevik revolution. He committed suicide when he learned he had cancer.

Fanny Baron: Fanya Baron, Russian anarchist, executed by the Bolsheviks on September 30, 1921.

Mahkno: Nester Mahkno (1889–1935), Russian anarchist, who led the revolt against the German occupation of the Ukraine during World War I. The Bolsheviks eventually purged Mahnko and exiled in Paris he died in poverty, obscurity, and bitterness.

A Lesson in Geography
"of Paradys ne can I speken . . .": From *The Travels of Sir John Mandeville*, a mid-fourteenth century account of the East. Originally written in French, it was translated into English, Latin, and German.

Boötes: the "plowman," a constellation.

"Moonlight on ruined castles" / Kojo n'suki: Title in English and Japanese of a poem by Doi Bansui (1871–1952), pseudonym of Tsuchii Rinkichi. It was set to music by Taki Rentarō and made famous.

from THE PHOENIX AND THE TORTOISE (1944)

Plutarch's page . . . Agis, Cleomenes: Plutarch (*c*. A.D. 46–c. *120*), Greek biographer and moral philosopher. His *Parallel Lives* relates the lives of eminent Greek and Roman statesmen and soldiers. Agis and Cleomenes were kings of Sparta in the second century B.C., and they are usually paired nineteenth in Plutarch's *Lives*.

existence / And essence . . . Of Aquinas: St. Thomas Aquinas (*c*. 1225–74), Italian scholastic, Dominican friar, and Christian theologian.

Ptahs: Ptah in Egyptian mythology is the creator and chief god of Memphis, and the father of Ra, the sun.

Jacob struggled . . . another name: Jacob, having wrestled with an angel, was given the name of Israel (Gen. 32:24–28).

the rose / Outlives Ausonius, Ronsard, / And Waller: Decimus Magnus Ausonius (*c*. 310–95), Roman poet born in Bordeaux; Pierre de Ronsard (1524–85), French lyric poet, the principal figure in the "Pléiade"; Edmund Waller (1606–87), English poet. The rose is a frequent image in their poetry, but see especially, Ausonius, *De rosis nascentibus*; Ronsard's sonnets "Comme on voit sur la branch au mois de May la rose" (*Les Amours*), "Quand vous serez bien vielle, au soir à la chandelle" (*Sonnets pour Hélène*), and *Ode à Cassandre*; Waller's "Go, lovely Rose!"

Horace: (65–8 B.C.), Roman poet. Cf. "I have built me a monument more lasting than bronze" (*Odes*, Book III, XXX, line 1).

Christopher Wren: (1631–1723), English architect, designer of St. Paul's Cathedral.

Richelieu: Armand Jean du Plessi, Duc de Richelieu (1585–1642), French statesman and chief minister to Louis XIII.

Whymper . . . "About 6 PM . . .": Edward Whymper (1840–1911) was the first to climb the Matterhorn in 1865. During the descent four members of the climb fell to their deaths. Account quoted by Rexroth is from Whymper's book, *Scrambles Among the Alps in the Years 1860–69.*

When We With Sappho
". . . about the cool waters . . .": Rexroth's translation of Sappho's apple tree fragment.

Lute Music
All the bright neige d'antan people: The refrain to François Villon's (1431–*c.* 1463) "Ballade des dames du temps jadis" ("Ballad of the Ladies of Bygone Times") in *The Testament* is "Mais ou sont les neiges d'antan?" ("But where are the snows of yesteryear?").

"Blithe Helen, white Iope, and the rest": Iope is the wife of Theseus or Aeolus' daughter.

from THE SIGNATURE OF ALL THINGS (1950)

Lyell's Hypothesis Again
Lyell, *Principles of Geology:* Sir Charles Lyell (1797–1875), leading geologist of early to midVictorian Britain. His greatest contribution to the field was to prove that the landscape of Earth's surface (e.g., mountains) is produced over millions of years, often imperceptibly, by natural processes, thus refuting the "catastrophic" theory of change. His work influenced Darwin. *The Principles of Geology* was published in 1830–33.

Nessus' shirt: The shirt dipped in the blood of the centaur Nessus, which when worn by Hercules caused him unbearable pain, and led to his death.

Delia Rexroth
Michael Field's book, *Long Ago:* Michael Field is the psuedonym of Katharine Harris Bradley (1846–1914) and Edith Emma Cooper (1862–1913). *Long Ago* (1889) is a volume of poetry in which fragments by Sappho were expanded into poems.

Andrée Rexroth
Henry King's *Exequy:* Henry King (1592–1669), bishop of Chichester and author of verses sacred and profane. "An Exequy to his Matchlesse never to be forgotten Friend" was written on the occasion of the death of Ann King, his wife.

Yuan Chen's great poem: Possibly an allusion to "Three Dreams at Chiang-ling" by the Chinese poet Yuan Chen (779–831), which describes the dreams of a husband for his dead wife, usually understood as referring to the poet and his wife.

Isar: River in Austria and Germany, which bisects Munich and flows into the Danube.

A Letter to William Carlos Williams
Brother Juniper: One of the original followers of St. Francis of Assisi (1182–1226).

The girls of the Anthology: *The Greek Anthology* is a collection of approximately 6,000 short elegiac poems, epigrams, etc., by more than 300 writers from the 7th century B.C. to the 10th century A.D.

Anyte: Greek poetess, active *c.* 290 B.C., whose verses are included in *The Greek Anthology.*

George Fox: (1624–91), founder of the Society of Friends, or Quakers. His *Journal,* published in 1694, narrates his spiritual experiences and the persecutions of his followers.

from THE DRAGON AND THE UNICORN (1952)

The plow in the furrow, Burns: Robert Burns (1759–96), Scottish poet. See "To a Mouse: On Turning her up in her Nest with the Plough, November 1785."

Chiron: Centaur who taught Achilles and many other heroes of Greek mythology.

What Marvell meant by desarts . . . : Andrew Marvell (1621–78), English metaphysical poet. See "To His Coy Mistress."

Die Ausrottung der Besten: German; "the extermination of the best."

Stink of Papacy: The curia resided in Avignon beginning with Pope Clement V in 1309, until Gregory XI re-established it in Rome in 1377. During the papal schism (1378–1417), two anti-popes, Clement VII and Benedict XII, resided in Avignon.

Fromentin: Eugene Fromentin (1820–76), French painter and novelist, best known for his pictorial scenes of Algeria and his novel, *Dominique.*

King René: René of Provence (1408–80), known as "le bon Roi René," son of Louis II, duke of Anjou, and titular king of Naples, the Two Sicilies, and Jerusalem.

author of *Le Rideau levé* / Approached . . . by / Sade: Honoré-Gabriel de Riqueti, comte de Mirabeau (1749–91), orator and statesman in the National Assembly, and author of *Le Rideau levé ou l'Education de Laure* (*The Raised Curtain or the Education of Laura*). Mirabeau was jailed in Vincennes in 1777, where he quarreled with the Marquis de Sade (1740–1814), who had been jailed for having given prostitutes candy laced with the aphrodisiac Spanish fly.

Granet painting in Rome: François Marius Granet (1775–1849), French painter, born and died in Aix-en-Provence, went to Rome in 1802. Granet established a museum in Aix which bears his name, and in which hangs his portrait of Ingres (French painter, 1780–1867) and his *Un quart-d'heure avant l'office* of a dying man.

Milhaud: Darius Milhaud (1892–1974), born in Aix-en-Provence, French composer, one of "Les Six," and especially known for his development of polytonality and uses of American jazz.

Deux Magots: Literary and artistic café in Paris on the Boulevard Saint-Germain, since the 1920s.

Boswell: "Sir, what is the chief / Virtue?" . . . : Adapted from James Boswell's *Life of Johnson* (Wednesday, April 5, 1775): "Johnson: . . . Whereas, Sir, you know courage is reckoned the greatest of all virtues; because, unless a man has that virtue, he has no security for preserving any other."

Simone Martini: (*c.* 1284–1344), Sienese painter.

Bronzino: Agnolo Bronzino (1503–72), Florentine painter, court painter to Cosimo I de' Medici and important Mannerist portrait painter.

Taddis and Gaddis: Taddeo Gaddi (*c.* 1300–*c.* 1366), Florentine painter. There is no painter by the name of Taddi, though there is another contemporary painter of the name Bernardo Daddi (*c.* 1290–1349). Both were pupils of Giotto.

Masaccio: Tómmaso di Giovanni di Simone Guidi, known as Masaccio (1401–*c.* 1428), Florentine painter, who advanced the art of perspective.

Shekinah: A word used frequently in Jewish mysticism to mean the immanent principle, feminine aspect of God. (Hebrew meaning, "that which dwells or resides.")

The sephiroth of the Kabbalah: The sephiroth are the ten attributes or emanations by means of which the Infinite enters into relation with the finite.

the chakras of the Tantra: The *Tantras*, Sanskrit religious books (6th and 7th centuries A.D.), form the basis of a Hindu cult whose adherents worship Shiva's wife, Parvati, the female spirit. The *Tantras* are mostly in the form of dialogues between Shiva and Parvati and contain one of the most elaborate spiritual systems in the whole of Hindu tradition. *Tantra* is Sanskrit for thread or warp, and *chakra* a spinning wheel.

Hafidh: Hafiz (1325–89), Persian lyric poet.

Rumi: Maulānā Jalāl-uddīn Rūmī (1207–73), greatest Sufi poet of Persia.

St. Theresa: St. Theresa of Avila (1515–82), Spanish Carmelite nun, famous for her mystical writing and visions.

144

Agathias Sholasticus: A Greek poet and historian in the age of Justinian (5th century A.D.), of whose reign he wrote a history in five books.

Filippino's / Weary lady: Filippino Lippi (*c.* 1457–1504), Florentine painter and son of Fra Lippo Lippi. His painting *Apparition of the Virgin to St. Bernard* (1486) is in the Badia in Florence.

"Too many nakeds for a chapel,"/Said Evelyn: John Evelyn (1620–1706), principally remembered by his *Diary*, which describes his travels on the Continent. Quotation probably a reference to Evelyn's comments on the Sistine Chapel: "Now we came into the Popes Chapell, so much celebrated for the Judgement painted by M: Angelo Buonarti . . . of vast designe and miraculous fantasy, considering the multitude of Nakeds, & variety of posture." (January 18, 1645)

Benjamin West: (1730–1820), American painter.

Says Evelyn, "Turning to the right . . .": See Evelyn's *Diary*, February 23–24, 1645.

Cineasti and Milioni: Italian, "film makers and the millions."

"La mauvaise conscience . . . 'denature.' " / So Bakunin says: Mikhail Aleksandrovich Bakunin (1814–76), chief proponent of nineteenth-century anarchism, prominent Russian revolutionary, and antagonist of Marx. Bakunin believed in the virtues of violence and the value of terrorism. Quotation translates from the French as, "The bad faith of the bourgeois, I have said, paralyzed the entire intellectual and moral movement of the bourgeoisie. I correct myself and replace the word 'paralyzed' by another: 'falsified.' "

"The bourgeoisie, wherever . . .": See Marx and Engels, "Bourgeois and Proletarians," *Manifesto to the Communist Party*.

For Dante / Usury was . . . its heirs: See *Inferno*, Cantos XV, XVII, and XVIII.

The Taoist uncut block: The uncut block represents the concept of man's original nature, free of all hostility and aggressiveness, inherent in newborn infants.

"A, E, I, O, U—the spheres . . .": See Arthur Rimbaud's (1854–91) Symbolist poem, "Voyelles" ("Vowels"), in which the vowels are given colors: A black, E white, I red, O blue, U green.

Japan, the goddess / Of the sun: The sun goddess, Amaterasu Ōmikama, holds the highest place in the Shintō pantheon and is the progenitor of the imperial line in mythology.

The doctrine of Signatures: The philosophical system of the German mystic Jacob Boehme (1575–1624).

The Smaragdine Tablet: The *Smaragdine Table* is a medieval Latin work on alchemy (published 1541), attributed to the Egyptian Hermes Trismegistus.

"The children have put purple . . .": A dedicatory epigram by Anyte from *The Greek Anthology*.

pronaos: Greek, "church vestibule."

naos: Greek, "church."

Bashō's frog: Matsuo Bashō (1644–94), Japanese haiku poet. A well-known and often translated haiku of his is:
> An old pond—
> The sound
> Of a diving frog.

Shiva: In Hindu mythology, Shiva represents the destructive principle in life and also the power of reproduction.

from THE LIGHTS IN THE SKY ARE STARS

A *Living Pearl*
"It is as though . . . itself uncleft.": Dante, *Paradiso*, Canto II.

from MARY AND THE SEASONS

Mei Yao Chen's poems: (1002–60), Chinese poet under the Sung dynasty. Mei's wife died in 1044 at the age of thirty-six, and two of his children died as infants. Their deaths moved him to write some of the finest poems of personal emotion in Chinese literature.

Thou Shalt Not Kill

I

Lawrence: St. Lawrence, martyr, charged with the care of the poor, was summoned by the Roman governor to deliver up the church's treasures, and he delivered his poor. Lawrence was roasted on a gridiron.

II

Leonard: William Ellery Leonard (1876–1944), American poet, essayist, and teacher, whose autobiography was entitled *The Locomotive-God* (1927).

Timor mortis conturbat me: Refrain to the poem "Lament of the Makaris," by William Dunbar, a Scottish Chaucerian poet (*c.* 1460–*c.* 1520), which translates from the Latin as "The fear of death troubles me." The "Lament" records a litany of dead poets ("makaris"), beginning with Chaucer.

Jim Oppenheim: James Oppenheim (1882–1932), American poet and novelist, who lived in Greenwich Village. He died of tuberculosis.

Lola Ridge: (1871–1941), Irish-born poet, came to the United States from Australia in 1907. Editor of *Broom*, she was active in the defense of Sacco and Vanzetti.

bird of Rhiannon: In Welsh mythology, Rhiannon had three birds who, singing, could bring the dead to life or likewise kill.

mains etendues: French; "outstretched hands."

Ignacio the bullfighter: The subject of Federico García Lorca's poem "Lament for Ignacio Sanchez Mejias."

Bran: The dog of Fingal in James Macpherson's (1735–96) Ossianic poem "Temora."

Taliesin: Welsh poet, a semimythical figure, who reputedly was the leading bard of the 6th century.

from THE HEART'S GARDEN, THE GARDEN'S HEART (1967)

II

Kant on Euler's bridges / Of dilemma in Koenigsberg: Immanuel Kant (1724–1804), German philosopher, born and died in Königsberg. Leonhard Euler (1707–83), Swiss mathematician, whose greatest discovery, the law of quadratic reciprocity, is an essential part of modern number theory.

uguisu: Japanese bush warbler, known for its beautiful song. The bird frequently appears in Japanese poetry and art as a motif paired with bamboo, willows, cherry trees, or pine.

Nishikigi: In Japanese "nishiki" is a profusely decorated silk brocade cloth, used as a costume in Noh plays. Furthermore, "nishikigoi" is a highly prized carp.

The Three Jewels: The Buddha, the Dharma, and the Sangha.

St. John of the Cross said it, / The desire for vision . . . : St. John (1549–91), Spanish mystical writer and Carmelite friar.

VI

The Eve of Ch'ing Ming: "Clear Bright," the Chinese festival of the dead.

pachinko balls: Japanese pinballs.

Chidori: Japanese plovers.

Kannon: Popular bodhisattva in Japan, the personification of infinite compassion. When the name Kannon, meaning "the one who hears their cries," is invoked, one is supposed to be delivered from danger.

from NEW POEMS (1974)

La Vie en Rose
La Vie en Rose: French song from the fifties with lyrics by Edith Piaf (1915–63) and sung by her. The title translates as "Life Through Rose-colored Glasses."

from THE SILVER SWAN (1978)

XIV
Hototogisu—horobirete: "The Japanese cuckoo—perishing."

from THE HOMESTEAD CALLED DAMASCUS (1920–25)

I
"ineluctable modality": ["of the visible"], from James Joyce's
Ulysses.

Tammuz: Sumerian god who died each year and rose again in the
spring. Identified with Adonis in Greek mythology.

II The Autumn of Many Years
Enoch: Sixth in descent from Adam and father of Methuselah.
Two apocryphal works are ascribed to him, *The Book of Enoch*
and *The Book of the Secrets of Enoch.*

Didymus: Greek word meaning "twin," which was applied to St.
Thomas, as the name Thomas derives from the Aramaic word for
"twin."

Baldur: Norse god of light, son of Odin and Frigg.

Modred: nephew of King Arthur, who turned traitor to Arthur
and was killed by him in battle.

Loki: Norse god of strife and spirit of evil. Loki contrived the
death of Baldur.

III The Double Hellas
Chloris: A girl to whom Horace addresses one of his odes.

Bactrian Kings: Bactria was a kingdom, centered in present-day
Afghanistan, which flourished from 600 B.C.–A.D. 600 and was the
crossroads for East and West.

Pisanello: Antonio Pisanello (*c.* 1395–1455), early Renaissance
Italian painter and medalist.

from A PROLEGOMENON TO A THEODICY (1925–1927)

Scala: Latin; "steps" or "ladder."

scholia: Latin; "academy."

Lux lucis: Latin; "light of light."

Et fons luminis: Latin; "and the fountain of light."

Tris agios: Greek; "thrice holy."

INDEX OF TITLES AND FIRST LINES

Poem titles are printed in *italic* type.

151